ENDORSEMENTS

Dr. Tau is one of the most knowledgeable marketing experts in the dental industry. He knows how to make patients your best advocates, online and offline. His strategies not only work, but they are also simple and do not add hours and hours to implement.

—**Margy Schaller,** *President, Laser Pointer Presentations*

I have known Dr. Len Tau for years. Watching him speak, stay up on technology, and share his knowledge with others is priceless. As a dental business coach and working inside dental practices for over 30 years, I can truly say that getting reviews is the No. 1 way to authentically gain new patients. His strategies for getting found by potential patients just plain work. *Raving Patients* should be required reading for all dentists in private practice. In addition, Len is a great guy!

—**Heidi Mount,** *Dental Coach*

The strategies for finding patients that The BirdEye Guy, Dr. Len Tau, teaches in *Raving Patients* will not just change your practice. They will change your life. Imagine having dozens of new patients coming to your practice every month without having to spend thousands of dollars on expensive and inefficient marketing. That could be your life if you implement Len's teachings in your practice.

—**Dr. Glenn Vo, DDS,** *creator of NiftyThriftyDentists.com, and co-founder of Dental* ___

When I first met Dr. Tau, I knew he had discovered something truly special to help with one of the biggest marketing challenges for dentists. His strategies for building and marketing a positive reputation online can help any dentist rise up in Google's search results and regularly attract new patients.

—Susan Leckowicz, *Dental Coaches*

Dr. Len Tau's strategies for getting found by patients just plain work. *Raving Patients* should be required reading for all dentists in private practice.

—Minal Sampat, RDH, dental consultant

Dr. Leonard Tau understands what it takes to get found online, build social proof, and market dental practices using reputation marketing strategies. I would highly recommend *Raving Patients* to any dentist looking to grow their practices.

—Joanne Block Rief, DDS

Raving Patients is the book I wish I had when I first opened my practice. It would have saved me a lot of time and money. No matter where you are in building your practice, this book can help.

—Dr. Maria Galdiano, Galdiano Dentistry

Raving Patients is packed with the latest strategies for getting more patients to come to your practice. If you are looking to grow your practice through reliable and proven strategies, this will show you the way.

—Jim Richardson, Founder/CEO, Click-Thru Consulting

I have followed Dr. Tau's teaching for a number of years. There is no better way to get found by patients online in such a compelling way. His methods are simple and reliable. They can truly help you get more patients by spending less time and money marketing than the normal practice. There is no other place I know that can make that claim.

—Pete Johnson, Cofounder, Get Practice Growth

The strategies in *Raving Patients* work so well because they match the exact process patients go through to find dentists. Dr. Tau's reputation marketing works better, faster, and at a lower cost because Dr. Tau goes over WHAT, WHY and HOW in a congruent manner that leads to effective (and lower cost) marketing.

—Tuan Pham, DDS

Raving Patients

RAVING PATIENTS

★★★★★

THE DEFINITIVE GUIDE TO USING
REPUTATION MARKETING TO ATTRACT
HUNDREDS OF NEW PATIENTS

DR. LEN TAU

NEW YORK

LONDON • NASHVILLE • MELBOURNE • VANCOUVER

Raving Patients

The Definitive Guide To Using Reputation Marketing To Attract Hundreds Of New Patients

Published in New York, New York, by Morgan James Publishing. Morgan James is a trademark of Morgan James, LLC. www.MorganJamesPublishing.com

ISBN 9781642797817 paperback
ISBN 9781642797831 hardcover
ISBN 9781642797824 eBook
Library of Congress Control Number: 2019913225

Cover Design by:
Andrej Semnic
www.behance.net/semnic

Interior Design by:
Chris Treccani
www.3dogcreative.net

Morgan James is a proud partner of Habitat for Humanity Peninsula and Greater Williamsburg. Partners in building since 2006.

Get involved today! Visit
MorganJamesPublishing.com/giving-back

DEDICATIONS

To Risa and Aidan:

Thank you to my amazing wife and son. You inspire me to work hard every day. Without your sacrifices, love, and support, I would not be able to do what I do. Thanks for always believing in and supporting me. I love both of you very much.

To My Dad:

Thank you for laying the groundwork for me to follow in your footsteps and become a dentist. Your passion for your craft and quest for clinical expertise inspired me to become a better clinician. You taught me how to be passionate about something and consistently be a hustler, things I have embraced myself. You drive me to do better all the time. I love you, Dad.

To My Mom:

Taken way too early, I think about you every day and know you are looking down and are proud of what I have accomplished.

To my amazing team at the Pennsylvania Center for Dental Excellence:

Alex Miller, Michele Quillen, Rossmery Hernandez, Melissa Linn and Audrey Su DDS, thanks for being the best of the best, allowing me to be away from the office doing the other things I love. I could not do it without your dedication and help.

To Dr. Don Katz:

You laid a strong foundation for your practice before your untimely death. I work hard every day to honor the legacy you left at Pennsylvania Center for Dental Excellence.

TABLE OF CONTENTS

Dr. Anissa Holmes

I've been a practicing dentist since 1999. For the first twelve years, I had a decent business and good relationships with patients. But in 2011, I came to the realization that I wanted more for my practice. I had a big vision. I wanted to grow and make a big impact in people's lives.

I immediately started working with my team and a business coach to help me turn my vision into reality. Three years later, I had achieved my big vision. My new-patient numbers increased tenfold, with practice revenue increasing by 300%! I even built a new state-of-the-art office without borrowing a penny.

Even more important than the numbers were the lives my team members and I were able to impact with our new focus and direction. My life was changed. My family's lives were changed. And my team members' and patients' lives were changed.

After transforming my practice, I started helping other practices do the same, starting with a podcast and my book, *Delivering WOW*, and eventually growing into monthly practice growth challenges, Facebook and business bootcamps, and my Delivering WOW Platinum Coaching program.

I've helped thousands of dentists develop a vision for their practice and take action to make their vision a reality. To do so, each of them put together a plan, put in place an amazing practice culture and patient experience, systematized operations, and invested in marketing to attract new patients. I also assembled a list of the best resources and experts in the dental industry to help practice owners in all the most important parts of building an efficient, profitable practice.

From the very beginning, one of the experts I have been recommending to clients is Len Tau. Len's passion and experience for reputation marketing is unmatched. From search engine optimization to website strategies, online reviews, and more, Len knows exactly how to get a dental practice noticed online in such a way that attracts new patients.

The secret to what makes Len's reputation marketing strategies so effective is they match the patient journey. Len's been practicing dentistry for years and knows what attracts patients to a practice and the path they take to get there.

Specifically, when a patient is looking for a new dentist, they often search online for dentists in their area for something like "best dentist" followed by their city or town. Or, they might search for their city or town followed simply by the word "dentist." Len's reputation marketing strategies help you reach the top of the search results when they conduct searches like those.

Once potential patients find you, they often look for patient reviews to see what others are saying about you before they decide to make an appointment. If they *don't* see reviews, they often move on. If you have recent, regular, and positive reviews, they are much more likely to call and make an appointment. The same is true even for word-of-mouth referrals. Patients often research dentists online before making an appointment, even if their friends and family recommend you.

Our need to build a comprehensive, positive online footprint is only getting more important as more and more people are looking online before choosing their next dentist. Thus, no matter how amazing an experience people have at your practice, you *must* build a robust, positive online presence to maximize the return on your investment. And there's no better person to help you do just that than Len Tau.

Len's reputation marketing strategies help you get your practice in front of patients exactly when they're searching for a dentist. They ensure potential patients like what they see when they find you. And, best of all, they will help you create an online footprint that builds trust with patients even before they come to your office. In the end, you will be able to regularly attract new patients to your practice who are much more likely to trust you and accept your treatment plans.

One of the biggest reasons I have dedicated so much of my time to helping practice owners build better, more efficient, and more profitable practices is to make dentistry more profitable, impactful, and fun. The strategies Len teaches in *Raving Patients: Your Playbook to Build A Five Star Reputation that Attracts Hundreds of New Patients* are an essential part of a holistic approach to doing just that.

Dr. Anissa Holmes
Top 25 Women in Dentistry
Social media strategist, author, and podcaster helping dentists create wealth and time freedom.
DeliveringWOW.com

PREFACE

Your happy patients are your most valuable asset.

Before you read this book, let's make sure it is right for you.
Do any of these statements fit you or your business?

- You are looking to enhance your online presence.
- You want more new patients but don't necessarily want to spend a lot of money getting them.
- Negative reviews have appeared online about your practice.
- Your competition has more patients, makes more money than you, or looks better online than you.
- You have a ton of happy patients and want them to talk about you online.
- You want to make more money.

If any of these describe you or your business, you're in the right place. But these are only a few of the reasons to read this book. There are too many to list here but they all point to one thing, which I call reputation marketing.

Reputation marketing is the most important and relevant way to market a dental practice, or almost any business for that matter.

Reputation marketing helps you leverage the power of feedback from happy patients to do each one of the things described in the bullet points above.

When dentists understand how critical it is to leverage feedback from happy patients for business success, they stop asking me whether they can afford to ditch the old way of marketing, and our conversation shifts to whether they can afford not to.

I have spoken to thousands of dentists over the years, either at my own seminars, on personal software demonstrations, or at other people's events. I've heard *every* cockamamie excuse under the sun for why reputation marketing won't work for a specific practice.

I've heard:

- "My patients don't leave reviews."
- "Most of my patients come from word of mouth."
- "My patients aren't on Instagram or Facebook."
- "I have too many new patients already."
- "I don't have the team to do it."
- "I don't have the time to do something new."
- "My patients are old."
- "My patients don't have a Gmail address or Google account"
- and many more

When dentists learn how much easier, more effective, and more affordable reputation marketing is compared to their existing ways, however, their sentiment usually changes pretty quickly. If you're concerned about any of those issues, invest a little time reviewing this comprehensive reputation marketing plan and I am confident you'll feel differently at the end, too.

How We Shop

What did you do before the last time you made a purchase, ate at a restaurant, went to a new movie, or visited a doctor?

Odds are, you went online and checked out what others said about the product, restaurant, movie, or doctor before making a final decision to buy, eat, watch, or schedule an appointment.

In a 2018 survey, marketing platform and search engine optimization (SEO) expert BrightLocal found that 86% of consumers (and 95% of those aged 18 to 34) read online reviews to determine whether a local business is a good one. That means only 14% do not. In other words, if you ignore reviews, you're directing your marketing to 14% of consumers and ignoring 86% of them. It's like placing a full-page ad in the Yellow Pages—which only 7% of the population goes to. You need to hit the 93% who use the thing we call the internet.

BrightLocal also found that 78% of consumers trust online reviews as much as personal recommendations (91% in consumers aged 18–34). Thus, if you ignore reviews, you're ignoring an opportunity to build trust with potentially 91% of the people looking for a dentist. When people trust you, they trust your treatment plans. They buy from you. They open their wallets. They spend money. It does not get better than that.

Do this before reading any further.

Now that I (ideally) have your attention, I want you to try something before moving to the next section. This might sound strange, but I can't tell you how many dentists I meet who have never done this or even knew this.

Put yourself in the shoes of a potential patient looking for a dentist. Open a *private* web browser, called an "Incognito Window" in Google's Chrome browser or a "Private Window" in Apple's Safari browser. Make sure your browser is a private one because it ensures your results won't be skewed by your past web history. Web browsers and search engines get to know you based on your past activities, so they return different information to you than they would to a patient who has never looked at your webpage, social media accounts, etc.

For example, many times when I talk with doctors or team members, they tell me that they always rank on page one of Google. When I look them up, however, they are far down on the list. What are they using to search? They tell me their browser in the office or their cell phone. If you do this on a consistent basis, Google will show the most relevant rankings, which is your office. This is not necessarily what your potential patients are seeing on their computer or phone. It's important to use a private window in order to see what patients see.

Open Google and run a search for "dentist" and your town. Are you one of the three offices listed in the big map that shows up right below the paid ads, which is called the "map pack"? If not, click on the words "more places" on the bottom of the map pack and search for your business name.

Where are you located in the map pack? Are you even visible?

If not, how are potential patients going to find you if they're looking for a dentist in your town?

Next, I want you to do one more search, this time searching for your business name. How many Google reviews do you have? What other review sites come up on the first page? How many review sites come up? How many reviews do you have on those sites? Are all the sites on page one related to your office, or do you see other offices in your area listed there?

If you were a patient who came across your practice name and decided to do some research before considering making an appointment, would those results entice you to make an appointment?

If you didn't appear in the map pack and were nowhere to be found on the "more places" page, you are invisible to anybody searching for a dentist. And if you don't have regular, recent, positive reviews, nobody who *has* managed to find you will be enticed to make an appointment.

You *need* online reviews to attract more new patients to your practice. It's not optional anymore, especially if you're in a competitive area. You need to have a bunch of reviews just to be on an even playing field with your competition. But you need regular, *raving* reviews to stand out.

I call this "word-of-*mouse*" rather than "word-of-*mouth*" marketing because it all happens over the internet with a click of a mouse (or a trackpad) instead of in person with people talking to each other. You need visibility and credibly online to survive in a word-of-*mouse* world. Reputation marketing helps you achieve that.

"Reputation is important, reputation means revenue, and reputation matters."

—Dr. Len Tau

My Relationship with Reputation Marketing

I love online marketing. It's been one of my passions since I bought my dental practice in 2007, after associating in a practice in Lansdale, Pennsylvania, for almost six years. I knew that I always wanted to own my own practice but also wanted to hone my skills as a clinical dentist for a number of years before venturing out on my own.

My wife and I were expecting our son (who was born two months after I bought the practice), and I had a huge debt service to cover every month—$18,000 for my practice note and office renovation. I also needed to make enough to pay operating costs and take home enough to support my wife and newborn son.

It was my first time owning—and marketing—any practice. I had worked in some offices as an associate, but those practices never marketed much. They either took every insurance available or were near a large corporation, such as Merck, that flooded the office with new patients.

I had never even taken a marketing class in my life, which, upon reflection, might have been a good thing because it made me learn by doing. Some things flopped, but other things worked *really* well. My entire marketing knowledge came from going online and trying things.

More than a decade later, I'm now *teaching* dentists how to market their practice, sharing my best strategies for marketing dental practices.

What was my secret? It all boils down to two words:

Online reputation.

I grew my *entire* practice around building *and marketing* a five-star online reputation. Without that, I would not be where I am today, and thousands of dentists I've helped replicate my success would still be struggling, too.

I've tried every type of marketing you can imagine. By far, the most predictable, stable, and affordable way to market a practice is through reputation marketing.

The truth is, every dental practice *already* has an online reputation. The only question is whether it's an *asset* or a *liability*. If you have a consistent, professional online presence and a steady flow of legitimate and positive reviews, your online reputation is likely a big asset. If you have an inconsistent presence, no presence, negative reviews, old reviews, or no reviews, your online reputation is a liability because it's the first thing people see when searching for you online.

"It takes 20 years to build a reputation and five minutes to ruin it. If you think about that, you'll do things differently."

—Warren Buffett

Google displays your reviews prominently on the first page of results, so potential patients see your reviews before they even go to your site—or worse, as a colleague of mine recently discovered. A family with six children scheduled appointments only to cancel the next day. When asked the reason why, they told the dentist that they did not like what others said about her practice online. (By the way, she has 3.5 stars with 79 Google reviews). Can you imagine how many people never call your office and just move on to the next office? If they don't like what they see, they might never go to your site.

Of course, great reputation marketing is more than just collecting online reviews. It's also about creating great, fresh content. As we've all heard, content is king. Distributing reviews through social media and other forums is a great way to use those reviews as fresh content. Search engines love fresh content and reward sites that update regularly.

INDUSTRY INSIGHTS

The value and importance of reviews has never been so prevalent. As a coach for dentists who are trying to set themselves apart from other dentists, I know just how critical reviews are. When I talk to the administrative team members about new-patient phone training, I always ask them to ask the patients how they heard about the practice. More than 50% of the time, the patient mentions they read online reviews and decided to call. I also coach the team members to ask the patient, "Have you seen our online reviews?" and guide the new patient to look up reviews after they schedule their appointment. It is a tremendous way to grow trust with someone who is either nervous or unsure about the practice.

One of my dental-coaching clients has been using online reputation software for the past two years and has grown his Google reviews to over 115. He recently had a new patient agree to a $30,000 implant case at his initial appointment. The patient said the reviews really impacted his decision—not only the quantity but also the quality of what other patients wrote. He felt so confident he was in good hands.

I believe that dentistry truly changes lives. In the day to day of the practice, both the dentist and the team members often get discouraged by patient complaints, or upsets. Some patients are shy and express the gratitude they feel for the care through an online review. Many times team members don't want to focus on the numbers of running the business and feel that the focus shifts away from patient care. Having the ability to hear directly from patients is a great way to make everyone feel that they are making a difference.

—**Susan Leckowicz,** *Dental Coaches*

Each positive review you receive can act as unique content about your practice. The more you get, the more Google and other search engines see your practice as something people are interested in. So, garnering as many positive reviews on the sites that matter most allows review sites to populate page one of Google's search results and push other things—potentially negative comments—to page two, which might as well not exist.

Compare these two practices.

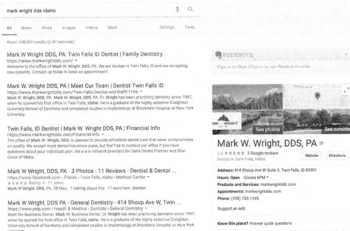

Which of the two practices would you be more likely to visit? It's an easy decision for many patients to choose the one with more people saying positive things about the practice and with the search results consisting of one appearance of the dental practice and a bunch of different review sites indicating patients all over the internet have rated the practice positively. I'll share more about this throughout the rest of the book.

Stop the Madness

Few things are as disappointing as having spent years honing your skills, building your practice, and developing a warm chairside manner only to have *one* unhappy patient or disgruntled employee rip you apart online.

Even worse, what if the person isn't even an actual patient or a disgruntled former employee? It happens. I won't debate you whether it's fair for online review sites to leave up factually incorrect reviews, or those clearly from someone who never visited your practice. Like it or not, these sites are not a fad—they are here to stay, and they're becoming even more important by the moment, as more and more people look for reviews before deciding to come in to your office.

But the problem isn't negative reviews deterring patients from your office. The problem is patients avoiding your office—without you even knowing about it. They don't come in and tell you they decided to go to another dentist. They just go to another dentist and move on. So, unless you're actively building and marketing your reputation, you have no idea *how* many patients you're losing.

I get about two dozen patients every month who tell me my online reviews convinced them to come to my office. It doesn't get much better than that. Have I mentioned I have more *negative* reviews than most practices have *total* reviews? It's true. I have more than 80 negative reviews online. But I also have more than 1,750 *positive* ones.

Getting bad reviews sucks. There's no sugarcoating it. But reputation marketing helps you make them less relevant. And I'll share exactly what to do about negative reviews in Chapter 8.

If you're spending a lot of money on Google Ads, social media marketing, and SEO, you're likely wasting a lot of money by driving traffic to an online presence that doesn't attract patients to your chair. That's a problem. Reputation marketing is your solution.

So if your online presence is negative or nonexistent, you're better off stopping all your marketing and focusing your efforts on building your online presence. Dentists who do so rarely go back to the old way of marketing. During my seminars I like to say, "Stop your marketing spend until you have a steady flow of authentic reviews, since you're wasting your money."

Okay, I'll get off my soapbox now about why I wrote this and what I want you to get out of this book. It's time for you to get started. In the next section, I'll reveal the best way to read this book to get the most out of it.

Hint: I'll tell some stories (as I do in my seminars for those who have seen me speak—if you have not but want to, visit DrLenTau.com to see where I am speaking next or how to book me for a speaking gig in your area), but it's not a novel. I want you to read and apply this book's info, and I will explain more in the next section. I'll then share a little more detail, including a bit more about my story, in a short introduction section that puts the rest of the plan into the right context for you so you can see how the topics in the rest of the book all work together as one comprehensive plan.

At the end of the day, the longer you wait, the longer it will take for you to stop relying on expensive and ineffective marketing.

What are you waiting for? Flip the page and get moving! Enjoy! My goal as you read this book is to take actionable items directly to your practice your next working day and understand the important value proposition of online reputation to have a thriving, successful practice.

HOW TO READ THIS BOOK

This book gives you a proven, three-part process to use reputation marketing to consistently attract new patients to your dental practice by leveraging the power of your existing happy patients.

I have taught this process to more than 20,000 dentists one-on-one, in small groups, and in large settings at conferences around the U.S. I have also consulted with hundreds of dental practices to help them grow their practice through online marketing. I have taken frantic phone calls from dentists who received less-than-stellar reviews and are freaking out. I have seen it all.

The dentists who get the best results from reputation marketing understand why the reason this process works is just as valuable as the specific steps to implement the process. When they examine each step and how it relates to their goals, their success skyrockets.

Because of that, my teaching is very hands-on. Unlike many speakers and trainers who ask people to silence their phones and put them away, I ask people to take out their phones, and I walk them through exercises to show them exactly why this is important and how to experience things as if they are potential patients looking for a dentist.

I am going to do the same for you in this book—not only walking you through the proven, three-step reputation marketing process, but also showing you why it works so well and sharing some exercises to help you experience how powerful this plan can be for your practice.

Getting The Most Value Out of This Book

As you are reading, stop and perform the exercises I give you at the end of each chapter before moving on to the next. Take notes, and write out your goals. Use the margins, separate sheets, or download the free reputation marketing goals and guidelines sheets I've created for you.

Doing so after each chapter will put the information you just read into a proper context and set you up to better receive the information from the following chapter.

To download the forms, visit DrLenTau.com/BookResources. You'll also see several other resources I refer to in this book there and be able to sign up to receive the latest reputation marketing updates by email.

While you're there, subscribe to *The Raving Patients* podcast, where I share even more tips for turning patients into *raving* patients, marketing a five-star online reputation, and building a practice you love. During the podcast, I interview some of the industry's most well-known guests, who share a few of their success stories.

Subscribing to the podcast ensures you stay up to date with all the latest reputation marketing strategies and rule changes. The internet changes every day, as does Google's algorithm. Use me and my podcast to stay up to date on the best and latest information to keep you compliant and reaping the internet's rewards.

Whatever you do, remember that your results come from your actions. This book won't do anything *for* you. It will only educate you. Your results will come from what you do with the information in this book.

The good news is you don't have to do it all yourself. You can delegate many tasks to team members. And even if you implement only a few of the things I recommend in here, you can still see a huge positive impact on your business.

So, feel free to identify the things you feel you can implement and wait to see the improvements happen. As you see things improve, add more. You can totally take it one step at a time. But to see results, you need to actually take *some* steps.

Unless you *implement* your education, you have only been entertained. Education without action is just entertainment.

While this book will certainly entertain you, my purpose in writing this book is to help my fellow colleagues finally take control of their online reputation and exponentially improve the return investment in marketing.

I wrote it to help you achieve the time and financial freedom that reputation marketing can bring.

I wrote it to help you destress and achieve the peace that comes when you no longer have to worry about where your next patient will come from, whether you will be able to pay your bills, or if you can afford to take time off for a much-needed vacation. We are all very busy running our practices, treating patients, and dealing with overhead— and this aspect should be something that does not cause undue stress.

But remember, that freedom doesn't come from reading. It comes from doing.

Do the exercises, and then implement the plan.

And if you need help or have any questions along the way, just email or call me.

You can reach me anytime at Len@DrLenTau.com or (215) 292-2100.

I **will** find the time to speak with you. I'm super responsive, as my patients and many of my clients will attest. But if for some reason you do not get a response, it's usually because I am working in someone's mouth, flying on a plane, or giving a seminar. Please be patient; I will get back to you ASAP.

I do have one request, though—if you ask for my advice, please take it. If you enjoy this book, please tell your friends and colleagues about both this book and my podcast (which is a great outlet for me to use to educate you, the reader).

And please remember that your reputation matters.

INTRODUCTION

How would it feel to almost effortlessly attract dozens of new, ideal patients to your dental practice each and every month?

What would it do for your practice if those new patients came in already trusting you, so you didn't have to constantly convince people to accept your treatment plans?

How would you like to have your practice naturally rise to the top of Google's search results without having to spend thousands of dollars on expensive search engine-optimization campaigns?

Finally, how would it feel to not have to worry that one unhappy and unreasonable patient could bring you down by posting a one-star review about you online?

All of that is possible with reputation marketing.

INDUSTRY INSIGHTS

I've owned my dental practice for 14 years and have always marketed my practice internally and externally. I try to create unique marketing ideas, sometimes even ideas that are outside the box. So when selfie sticks came onto the market, I ordered several dozen that were personalized with my practice name, and used them as an incentive when patients gave me a Google review.

Dr. Len Tau heard about the selfie sticks, and reached out to tell me there were better ways to get tons of Google reviews without bribing patients. I listened but did not make a move until a short time later. I ran into Len at The Chesapeake Dental Conference in Ocean City, Maryland. He explained how and why Google and Facebook reviews were so important to attract the right kinds of patients that I wanted in my practice.

At that time, I had 40 Google reviews, the third highest in my area. I told Len that I wanted to have the most Google reviews in my area, which meant I needed more than 100. Since following Len's advice on reputation marketing, I now have more than 450 Google reviews and plenty of great Facebook reviews.

One woman traveled close to an hour to our office after reading our reviews. She probably passed a hundred other dental offices on her way to our office. She said she was looking for a place that was not necessarily over the top or too pushy, just a nice atmosphere and a warm environment. Hundreds of people would not have been patients in my office if it were not for my fantastic reviews. Raving fans make the best dental patients!

—**Joanne Block Rief,** *Crossroads Dental Arts,*
Owing Mills, Maryland

How it All Began

In 2007, when I bought my dental practice, none of this was possible. Dental-practice online marketing was expensive and certainly not as effective as it is today. Practice-building took years of slow growth using traditional advertising such as phone book or newspaper ads, word-of-mouth patient recommendations, direct mail campaigns—which few recipients ever open—and building relationships with insurance plans. The website Yelp! had been around for a few years, and other review sites were gaining popularity. Patients could reach thousands of people by posting a review about your practice online, good or bad. That was an exciting but scary proposition for many dentists.

That is the environment I faced after purchasing my dental practice in 2007, from the estate of a dentist who had committed suicide. I had a new $18,000-per-month practice loan payment from not only buying a fee-for-service practice but also buying and remodeling the building to make it feel different—plus operating expenses and personal financial obligations.

I was pretty overextended financially and did not have thousands of dollars to pour into traditional advertising or the time to wait for word of mouth to spread. I had a practice to run. On top of that, the practice was in rough shape, as you might imagine with one that had been run by a dentist who tragically took his own life. I *did* inherit an amazing team who stayed with me after the purchase, but as you may expect, some of the patients of the previous dentist chose not to come back. Some that did come back did not mesh personally with me. Many others chose to come back and remain my patient. Learning to market my practice was a necessary step I had to take in order to survive.

Traditional dental marketing was expensive or ineffective, and patients were just starting to become active online. I tried to build the practice as best I could for the first couple of years, but it was a struggle. I wasted $30,000 on a radio campaign where the only thing I got was a half-season's worth of Phillies tickets and zero patients. (Okay, I did get one patient from that deal—the radio guy who sold me the package. He must have felt so badly about my getting zero patients that he actually became a patient himself. Many weeks, I did not take a salary instead choosing to reinvest the money to make the practice better, and I needed a better and more cost-effective way to attract new patients to my practice. I needed to market my practice without adding thousands of dollars in costs to the already-high operating expenses and debt service.

After searching everywhere for an answer, I recognized a gap between how people shopped for dentists and how dentists were marketing. Specifically, by that time, online reviews had become mainstream in many industries. Consumers routinely searched Google to find online reviews about a company before doing business with them. Even if a company were recommended by a friend, people would still look for reviews before moving forward. In the past, patients would just ask friends or family members for a recommendation, call the office, and make an appointment. I saw this firsthand as my dad, Morton Tau, an amazing mentor who also just happens to be a dentist in my hometown of New City, New York, did *zero* paid marketing of his practice. His was 100% a word-of-mouth practice—he put up a shingle, and the patients just came.

But as I discovered, I could not rely on word-of-mouth as my father had. Across industries, people were using *word-of-mouse*, from buying products to eating at a restaurant and even choosing a doctor or dentist. I'd seen my patients do this, and I had done the same as well. The problem I had, though, was I had virtually no online presence. My practice was barely visible online. I had been working as an associate in Lansdale, Pennsylvania—a suburb of Philadelphia—and previously in Mount Holly and Browns Mills, New Jersey, so there was a lot of incorrect information online as well. Not a great combination.

In these practices, one was heavily insurance based that did not market at all—the patients just came because he took every insurance under the sun, and he even did a lot of bartering. When I moved to Lansdale and a mostly fee-for-service practice, we were very close to Merck Pharmaceuticals, and the practice I worked at did little marketing as well.

When I purchased my practice, I teamed with a very well-known marketing company from DentalTown that helped me set up my logo and branding, my web presence, SEO, and even the brochures that

I gave out. I spent the next several years researching, studying, and searching for marketing solutions that would help me build a strong online presence, so when patients searched for a dentist in my area, they would both find me and decide that I was the right dentist for them.

I also wanted patients who went online to search for me after being referred to me by a relative or friend to want to make an appointment with me based on what they found online.

A 3-Part Plan That Would Revolutionize Dental Marketing

I knew I needed to accomplish three things if I wanted to market my practice this way. First, I needed to get found online. My practice needed to rank high on Google's search results. It was and still is the largest search engine in the world. That is where most people go to search for a dentist or look up reviews about them.

Second, I needed to get found in a compelling way. What potential patients saw when they found me online needed to encourage them to make an appointment with me.

Third, I needed a simple process to monitor and protect my online reputation. I needed a way to know what was being said about me online and a plan to protect myself against negative reviews.

After searching everywhere for a simple solution that would accomplish those three things, I came up blank. I tried so many platforms on the market back then, but they were either not comprehensive enough, too difficult, or simply did not do what they said they were going to do. It was super frustrating, and I knew that I needed to do something about it.

Even worse, there was not even any good place to learn about how to accomplish those three things. The only articles or posts I found were about *reputation management*. I did not need to *manage* my reputation. I had a good reputation. But I needed more potential patients to know about me.

In other words, I did not need to *manage* my reputation; I needed to *market* my reputation. That is much different. Reputation *management* is unfocused, reactive, and ineffective. It is an old term that makes me cringe. Even now, when I hear companies say they do reputation management, I want to bang my head against the wall.

In practical terms, reputation *management* is the process people take to try to bury or remove negative reviews. It's worrying about negative reviews and pushing negative stories off the first page of Google's search results. I call it reverse SEO. It does not work and will not help your practice. It is a waste of time and money. I have seen dentists waste thousands of dollars and dozens of hours trying to bury negative stories or remove negative reviews. The vast majority of times, it does not work. I'd rather you focus on filling up the first page of Google search results with positive reviews and other positive content. That's a reputation *marketing* strategy. And that can actually push negative things off the first page of Google's search results and attract new patients to your practice.

Reputation marketing is the focused, proactive, and effective practice of building and marketing a five-star online presence. Reputation marketing improves search rankings, encourages patients to visit your practice, and protects against potential negative reviews or stories posted about you online. Most importantly, it unlocks the door to be able to increase your marketing spend.

"A brand for a company is like a reputation for a person. You earn reputation by trying to do hard things well."

—Jeff Bezos

Reputation marketing is controllable. It is reputation management on steroids, and combines the most useful elements of reputation management with the most effective brand-marketing techniques. I wanted a reputation *marketing* solution.

That's why you'll see me refer to *reputation marketing* and not *reputation management* from now on. I don't want you to focus any time, money, or attention on reputation management. Spend that time on reputation marketing and getting happy patients to talk about you online—and let me help you leverage the *power of your happy patients*.

Be careful, as many scrupulous companies out there claim they can get negative reviews off the first page of Google—this is almost impossible and very unpredictable, so remember, you have been warned. If you are talking to a web company looking to help you with marketing and they refer to *reputation management*, I would hang up the phone and look to work with another company as this term is extremely out of date. Do a Google search for "dental reputation management" and see all the companies who are saying they do management of the reviews. There are some very well-known companies on these pages.

My Search for Automatic and Predictable Practice Growth

I started seeing the huge effect reviews had on my practice in 2009, when I started using a communication software program called Demandforce that collected reviews via email. Thanks to a relationship with Google, those reviews showed on the Google Local business listing. I attended trade shows on behalf of Demandforce and used to say, "They put you on the map." Dentists who used them had more reviews than any other office. At that point, reviews were something many dentists ignored, but I embraced them as I saw firsthand the effect they had on my practice. When I asked patients how they came to my practice, I heard more and more about online reviews. Clearly, this was important. I made a point to ask all patients how they heard about my office, and it's something I continue to do today—myself, without relying on my team.

It's great market research to learn what your patients were searching for, why they chose your office, and more.

As my review count increased, the phone calls increased, and patients said that the reason they chose my office was simply *my online reputation*. A lightbulb went on in my head—this was a *huge* differentiation factor. I decided to start getting my own Google reviews from patients just in case the relationship with Google ever ended with Demandforce. I started asking patients to write a review, and also explained to my team how important these would be for long-term success. I made reputation a culture in my office.

In July 2011, Google eliminated all third-party reviews from showing in the Google review total. Almost overnight, dentists went from having hundreds of reviews to fewer than 10, and sometimes zero. They literally lost their reputation. I, on the other hand, was proactive and started to ask patients for reviews, which, combined with the 25 Google reviews I already had on my own, proved to be a huge differentiator when comparing myself to other dentists.

After Google had essentially leveled the playing field, I set my sights on the perfect platform to help generate Google reviews for my office. I tried every possible way, even ways that are no longer allowed by Google—a kiosk in the office, incentivizing patients, other software programs—but some of them were too complicated, took too many steps, just did not work, or were against the terms and conditions that Google had at the time. (By the way, office kiosks and patient incentives are now officially against Google and Yelp!'s terms and conditions, so don't use them.)

It was a frustrating process, to be perfectly honest. As I started to speak around the country on the power of online marketing and its ability to attract new patients to one's practice, I heard that many of my colleagues shared that frustration. I knew I needed to do something. I knew where my calling was. I needed to build my own software. That is just what I did.

Having found no existing reputation marketing software solutions, I decided to build my own, and in 2013, I teamed up with a partner and a developer to create iSocialReviews as an offshoot of my consulting company, iSocial Dental Consulting. The first version of iSocialReviews was not a perfect solution, but it filled all the gaps in the market and helped me generate online reviews as well as market them while protecting against potential negative reviews.

After a significant testing and further development, I built iSocialReviews into the only comprehensive reputation marketing software in the market.

Here's a look at some of my own milestones and numbers.

In 2009, I had 279 new patients come to my practice. It was my third year at my practice. Most of my marketing in 2009 was pay-per-click (PPC) advertising, as well as differentiating myself from other dentists in the area. I would call new patients on the weekend and go with patients to their oral surgery consults and procedures. I would give patients my cell number and answer the phone. (Looking back, I would never recommend PPC until you have a steady flow of reviews in order to differentiate yourself from the competition) although I started testing reputation marketing that year as well. Given that, about 25 new patients a month was a pretty good number of new patients for a fee-for-service practice almost entirely reliant upon pay-per-click to attract new patients.

By 2010, my consulting and reputation marketing initiatives through other avenues had started taking shape. In 2010, I had 768 new patients, or 64 new patients a month. I was so busy that I did not take a single day off in 2010 other than major holidays. I did nothing different in 2010, but continued to build my online presence, add more online reviews, and focus a bit on being found online. I also became the first dentist in Philadelphia to offer Groupon as a way to attract new patients to one's practice. For my office, it worked amazingly well as we deliver a "wow" experience to our patients, but for others, it did not work as well. (I have continued to do a lot of the same to this day, and I'm always trying new things to find the latest and greatest new patient-attraction technique.)

I heard from other dentists that Groupon patients are only looking for a deal and will never come back; they are more apt to leave a bad review; they have no money, etc. Some definitely fit this mold and will never come back to the office. I treated these patients as full cash patients and gave them an incredible experience, which made them want to come back to the office. Just this past week, I saw two kids who needed more than $4,000 in fillings. After the dad met with me on the first visit, he decided to bring his youngest son and as well as himself to the practice as patients, and paid more than $5,000 on Care Credit. When I delved deeper into why he chose to stay in the office, he said that they loved what others had to say about the way they were treated. Chalk another new patient up to my online reputation.

In 2011, the numbers were similar, with 763 new patients and no days off. Then, 2012 also was much of the same, with 780 new patients and zero vacation. By that point, my reputation marketing plan was working almost *too* well. I had more business than I could handle and was burning out from dentistry. I was constantly in the office, even on the days I did not see patients, running the business of dentistry. I barely saw my family, and it was not what I had envisioned.

I could not do it anymore. I had other things I wanted to do with my life. I needed to cut back on office hours. I had discovered a dental-marketing plan that I felt at the time was better than any other on the market and developed software to implement it. It made marketing my dental practice almost too easy, and I wanted to help other dentists take the stress and worry of marketing off their minds. I also wanted time to relax and have fun with my wife and son.

At the beginning of 2013, I decided I would accept fewer patients so I could consult more and spend more time with my family. Still, my schedule remained full, and patients regularly poured in with between

480 and 525 new patients each year since then, depending on how many days I work. I now attend about 36 trade shows per year, speak dozens of times a year, and spend some much-needed time with my wife and son.

As I was determined to cut down my schedule in 2013, I decided to begin offering reputation marketing consulting services and access to iSocialReviews to other dentists. My first attempt to attract consulting customers was at the 2013 Yankee Dental Congress, where I set up a booth for the first time. I had no idea if anybody would be interested in purchasing this software, as I had only attended a trade show and had not been a vendor. To my excitement, 10 people immediately subscribed to use iSocialReviews with my help. I was pleasantly surprised. Shortly thereafter, 10 became 20, 30, 50, and 100. And 18 months after first offering iSocialReviews to others, 180 dental practices were using it to not only generate positive online reviews but also to attract great new patients to their practice on a regular basis.

After building iSocialReviews beyond just serving my practice, I also started speaking more frequently and writing articles for magazines. One article in particular I wrote for *DentalTown* magazine called "Yelp! Can Be Detrimental to Your Dental Practice" caught the attention of a large company called Bazarify, now known as BirdEye. They connected with me to see if we could work together.

I was already connected in the dental space, where BirdEye wanted to grow. Birdeye had a better platform and vision of growing their company to much greater heights, so it was the perfect fit. The also wanted my expertise on how to sell into the dental space. It was a great opportunity for me because I was running two companies at the time— iSocialReviews and my dental practice, which was a lot of work. I had considerable loans I was still paying back and could not devote my undivided attention to growing it much more.

I wanted to continue to serve my iSocialReviews consulting clients, but running two companies was not sustainable, so, in 2014, we negotiated a deal for BirdEye to acquire my clients from iSocialReviews and bring me on board to lead its dental vertical. This freed me up to focus on what I loved most: reputation marketing consulting and continuing to practice dentistry. BirdEye and I now help more than 7,000 dentists with their reputation marketing, and BirdEye's other vertical serves more than 35,000 businesses in other industries.

BirdEye is just one of many software companies tailoring their services to the dental profession. Here's a look for your reference.[1]

Company	Services
BirdEye	Reputation Marketing, Patient Interaction, All-In-One Patient Experience Software
Demandforce	Reputation Management and Communication Software
Doctible	Communication Software, Reputation Management
Doctor.com	Healthcare Marketing Automation
Legwork	All-In-One Patient Engagement Software

---

1   By the way, if you are looking for an online scheduling tool for your office that integrates with your practice management software, I personally use and recommend Local Med. It's not software that helps with reputation marketing, but a lot of people ask me about it, so I wanted to mention it here. To see how it works, check out my practice website, philadelphiapa.dentist. In addition for a special offer check out DrLenTau.com/BookResources.

Lighthouse 360	Communication Software
Modento	Patient Engagement, Communication, and Loyalty
Patient Activator	Communication Software
Podium	Patient Interaction Management
Revenue Well	Practice Marketing and Patient Communications
Social Review Wizard	Reputation Management
SolutionReach	Patient Relationship Management
Swell CX	Cloud Based Growth Platform for Businesses—Reviews, Feedback, and Insights
Weave	VOIP Phone Services, Communication Software, Basic Review Platform
Yapi	Practice Automation software— Patient Communication and Paperless Forms

In 2017, I hired an amazing associate dentist, Dr. Audrey Su, and in 2018, I was able cut back on my time on the office to two days per week. Today, I continue to work two days per week and spend the rest of my time consulting with dentists and dental practices and running

BirdEye's dental vertical, traveling between 35 and 40 weeks a year to seminars and trade shows. I'm doing what I love most: educating dentists on how to implement a reputation marketing plan for their practice that is not only more effective than traditional marketing, but also much more affordable. I have taught more than 20,000 dentists how to use reputation marketing to build their practices through seminars, consulting, and online learning platforms. Other topics I speak on include "Dominating Your Marketing Online," in which I teach dentists and teams how to attract new patients through online marketing.

Let me be clear before we move forward. Although I work for BirdEye and am extremely passionate about the software we built, I want to be very transparent that this book is *not* an outlet to sell our software. This book is full of content with no fluff so you can do everything you need to implement a full reputation marketing program for your office without ever *having* to use our software.

Our software can help automate and ensure consistency. It can save you time. But you don't *need* it (or any other software) to do anything in this book. If you have ever been to one of my seminars, this will make sense. If not, you might want to attend one. I speak dozens of times a year, all across the country. Visit the resources page at DrLenTau.com to find out where I'll be next. Come to one of my classes. I'd love to meet you. It will change your outlook on marketing, I guarantee it! And bring this book. I will gladly sign it for you. You never know if it will be worth something down the road. :)

Reputation Marketing Is More Important Than Ever.

Gone are the days where there's only one dentist per town, and everyone visits that practice. Every year, new batches of dentists flood the market, competing for the same batch of patients as you. At the same time, patients are more mobile and internet savvy than ever, and do not just choose the closest dentist to their home or office. Patients are also not as loyal as they used to be, and will leave to find a dentist who is cheaper, more convenient for them, and who provides what they feel is a better experience.

Because of this dynamic, dentists cannot be just dentists these days. They also need to be marketers. The key is to market in a way that is predictable and relates to how people actually choose dentists. A comprehensive reputation marketing campaign is the best way to do that—much better than direct mail, traditional advertising, a blog, or search-engine-optimization campaigns.

I am a huge fan of the show *Shark Tank*, and one of its best takeaways: *you have to know your numbers*. Some KPIs are production, collection, overhead, how much ROI you are getting from your marketing efforts, and even case acceptance. One of the best programs to track all of your information is Dental Intel, which integrates with your practice management software and will help analyze the data in your software. Find out more in the resources section on DrLenTau.com.

Reputation marketing helps you use what people are already doing—talking online—to direct new patients to your practice. It also helps you get noticed where people already are, on Google, Yelp! Instagram, Facebook, Healthgrades, and many more. Finally, it helps you stand out from other dentists by having your patients sing your praises in far greater numbers and on a continuous basis, so you can have the greatest volume of relevant and recent positive experiences posted about you.

One of the most studied generations is Millennials, a group on which Michael Fertik writes often in *Forbes*. Take it from Fertik that reviews are a safe haven of information: "Millennials don't trust advertising, celebrity endorsements, or any of the more traditional, one-way communications strategies," he writes. "They're even growing skeptical of 'influencers,' and are beginning to doubt their credibility. This skepticism is in large part due to the 'fake news' phenomenon that has plagued (and to some degree, powered) politicians and celebrities alike over the past few years. Such untrustworthy media banter has eroded trust among U.S. consumers—and Millennials are probably the most wary of us all. So how do you build trust with younger consumers online? With user-generated content—like reviews … Nearly all Millennials (97%) read online reviews before selecting a business, and 89% trust those reviews. And a recent UK study found eight out of 10 Millennials never buy anything without first reading a review."[2]

Since 2009, when I first started using reviews and reputation marketing to grow my practice, the impact of reputation marketing has exploded in growth for these reasons and more. The internet is more developed than ever, and more dentists have websites, social media accounts, Clickfunnels, and pay-per-click campaigns than ever before. That means there's more competition for top search engine results than ever before. Because of that, it is more necessary than ever to implement a proven formula for getting found online.

---

2   https://www.forbes.com/sites/michaelfertik/2019/02/14/how-to-get-millenials-to-trust-and-respond-to-your-advertising

Additionally, study after study confirms that building online reviews in a systematized way is critical to attracting new patients to a dental practice (and most other business, too). It matters where we focusing our reputation marketing, also. According to a recent ReviewTrackers study, 63.6% of consumers check reviews on Google before visiting a business.

People who search for you online will now read and see your patient reviews before they consider looking at your website, yet people spend thousands of dollars developing websites that people will never visit because they have no online presence outside of their sites. Remember those that are searching for your business are considered people. When they come in, they are patients. Let's remember that 78% of consumers said they trust online reviews as much as personal recommendations, according to a 2018 BrightLocal survey.

Recent studies also show that consumers even trust reviews from unknown users more than expert opinions and advertising, with 70% trusting unknown users compared to 27% who trust experts and 14% who trust advertising. More than 68% of patients say positive online reviews make more likely to use a business, according to BrightLocal.

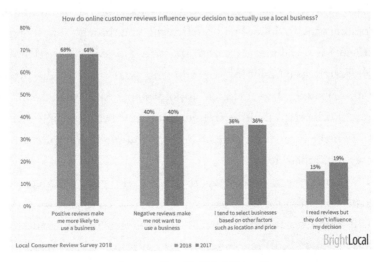

Image Credit: BrightLocal

These are just some of my reasons for saying that reputation marketing is the most important thing that you can do for your business. It's your most important asset, just like a credit score. A great credit score allows you many opportunities financially, while a great reputation help you significantly grow your business. A poor credit score limits your options, and a poor reputation will turn potential customers away.

Building a Simple Reputation Marketing Plan

This book teaches you the exact reputation marketing process I have used to attract hundreds of new patients to my practice each and every year, and the same process I have also used to help thousands of other dentists do the same.

First, I will walk you through a proven method for getting found online. This includes more than just generating reviews, although reviews are an important part of it. You need to also make sure your practice is listed properly everywhere Google looks to determine importance and relevance. I will show you how to do that. Finally, I will introduce the importance of reviews to getting found online.

Second, I will walk you through making sure you are found in a compelling way. To do so, I will briefly walk you through simple steps to effectively use social media for your practice. This will ensure that when people search specifically for you and find your social media profiles, they are encouraged to make an appointment. After that, I will give you the precise steps to use a simple online reviews campaign that will not only make it easier for patients to find you but also inspire them to choose you as their dentist.

I will teach you every step to do this in your practice, either manually or with software assistance from a company to make it virtually seamless. This is important because even if you decide to use software such as BirdEye, which makes collecting reviews automated, simple, and effective, you need to know the steps the software takes to help you. This will allow you to maximize the value of the reviews for your practice. I will walk you through everything you need to collect great online reviews, so when people find you, they will want you to be their dentist, they will come in, accept your treatment, say that magic word *yes*, and become your patients.

I will also show you how to handle negative reviews and why negative reviews can actually be a good thing for your reputation marketing plan. People are already talking about you online. When people have bad experiences, they talk about you online. That can turn potential patients away. Those negative reviews, if left alone, can be toxic to your practice.

"You can't build a reputation on what you are going to do."

—Henry Ford

Ignoring your online reputation is like throwing money away, because bad experiences that go unresolved will end up on the internet. That will turn into a bad reputation and cost you money, because the next people who find you online will move on to the next dentist. Remember, someone is not going to call your office and tell you they are not coming in as a patient because you suck online; they simply are going to bypass your office, and you will never have known what you have lost.

Think about that for a moment. You know that patients leave through the backdoor every month from attrition, but you have no clue about those people who simply choose another practice because you have no reputation or a bad reputation, or because another dentist has a better reputation than you. Let that sink in for a few minutes. Now, search online now for your closest competitor. Do they look better than you? How do you feel now?

This is one of my favorite topics to teach because many dentists fear negative reviews. Although they are still not something I actively solicit, I will show you how to make sure you are protected from negative reviews and what to do if someone posts one about you. A carefully nurtured and managed online reputation, however, can attract new patients and even turn negative reviews to a positive. As a recent study from SoftwareTracker reveals that spending just 10 minutes a week cultivating your online presence and managing feedback reduces the impact of negative reviews by up to 70%.

I will also show you how to seamlessly incorporate the collection of online reviews into your practice. Again, this is an area where software can simplify the process of soliciting and collecting reviews, speeding up the process of your practice showing up in a compelling way on search results, but it is important to understand the process as well. I will show you the process so you can get started right away, with or without software simplification.

Finally, I will help you monitor and protect your online reputation with a proactive marketing focus. The primary way you can accomplish this is by creating a reputation culture in your office. A reputation culture is the best way to benefit everyone involved in your practice, from your patients to team members and even you. I will show you exactly how to do this in your practice so your patients are happier and your employees are satisfied with their work. You will learn precisely how to monitor and build reviews as a natural part of your operations.

The Common Theme Underlying All Reputation Marketing

As you read through this book, you will notice an underlying theme: you must design your marketing to match how people choose dentists. Today, most people choose dentists based on search results and the dentist's or practice's online reputation. Reputation marketing presents you to people where they are looking, when they are looking, and in a way that lets them know you are the type of dentist they are looking for.

Reputation marketing also takes into consideration trends in the behavior of people and search engines. Specifically, people are spending more time on social media—an average of two hours and 22 minutes per day, according to a GlobalWebIndex study. They also prefer local companies by searching for terms such as "dentist near me," and are using cell phones to go online instead of using a laptop or desktop. A 2018 CIODive study shows that up to 70% of all online traffic now comes from smartphones.

In the reputation marketing world, we refer to this trend as "SoLoMo," which stands for social, local, and mobile. So, you will see that all of the methods I show you in this book are SoLoMo friendly. In fact, they are SoLoMo optimized. As you implement your reputation marketing plan, make sure you keep this theme top of mind so your plan is social, local, and mobile friendly. If you don't take this approach, you may end up becoming invisible rather than visible.

Correct citations are critical for more than just ranking. Consumers simply don't use a business if they find incorrect information.

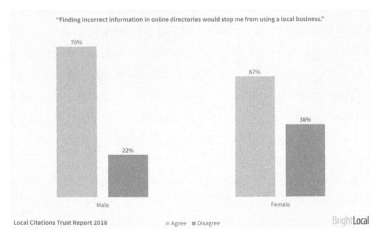

Image Credit: BrightLocal

On the other hand, clever language can help you take advantage of the "[blank] near me" trend, as we can see from this restaurant in Texas:

So, to improve your rankings, you could follow the restaurant's example and name your practice "Dentist Near Me!" I joke…

Are You Wasting Your Marketing Money?

The typical dentists I train come to me spending something north of $500 per month to a company that runs their website and does some form of search engine optimization. Even worse, some of these companies try to lock people into a long-term contract, forcing them to spend thousands of dollars to host and update their website and optimize it for search engines.

Whenever someone like this approaches me, I ask what the marketing company does to help their practice grow. Nobody knows. All they know is the company runs their website, fixes issues that arise, and does some sort of search engine optimization. I ask them what the ROI is, and they have no idea. I ask them what they are actually getting, and they have no clue. I just shake my head and wonder, *How can you be spending money on something and have no idea what you are getting in return?* I am sure some people are reading this and thinking to themselves, *I am in that boat.* If so, you are not the only one. Many others are just like you.

If this *is* you, ask the company to send you a list of what they are doing, along with a traffic report for your website. I recently came across a dentist who was paying several hundred dollars a month for this very service. I asked him to get me that information. The report indicated he had an average of 117 people visit his website each of the past three months. In other words, he was paying more than $4 per visitor to his website—and that's assuming every visitor came as a result of the marketing company's services. Those are horrible results. He might as well have not done anything.

In addition to the traffic report, his web company gave him a keyword report letting him know the most popular search people had done before coming to his site was "affordable dentistry." In other words, the web company was sending people who were looking for low-cost dental services and were unlikely to purchase elective or cosmetic services, or accept treatment plans that involved any significant out-of-pocket investment. Even worse, those patients were eating up his capacity to serve patients who would be more likely to purchase elective or cosmetic services and were better prepared and able to accept treatment plans even if they had to pay out of pocket.

After reviewing the rest of the documents, we realized he was wasting $500 per month. He promptly cancelled the service.

Another office showed me its report from a call-tracking software and its website company's report to go along with it. The website company was boasting about how many calls it was getting for the office. (The report was filled with so much boilerplate that it was hard to find the most important information unless you knew what you were looking for.) I looked at the key data: the length of an average call. It turned out to be 1 minute 8 seconds for all of their calls.

Let me ask you a question. What can possibly happen in that time frame? Not many appointments can be made, that's for sure. In addition, this website company put the same tracking number on every site on the internet. Let me repeat that. *They put the same tracking number on every site on the internet.* What are you actually tracking, then? Absolutely nothing. You want unique phone numbers on each of the major sites, including your website, so that you're able to track where your calls are coming from. Needless to say, this client cancelled services with this well-known company soon after speaking with me.

When I first started, I was in the same position as this dentist. I had been paying $600 per month for SEO services for five months and was still on the fourth page of search results. As many of us know, if you are not on the first page of search results, you might as well not be online at all. In fact, 75% of people do not make it past the first page of search results.[3]

I had no idea what they were doing and was not seeing *any* return on my investment, so I quickly cancelled, decided that SEO was not the best direction for my practice, and moved on to reputation marketing and looking for the best way to get reviews for my practice. There was no real way to quantify those results as well, so it makes it very difficult.

If you are spending $500 per month on SEO for a specific keyword, and after one year you are on page three, you just spent $6,000 and you have zero patients since you are not on page one. Not a good investment in my opinion. Remember the saying that goes, "The best place to hide a dead body is page 2 of Google search results because nobody goes there."

---

3   https://blog.hubspot.com/blog/tabid/6307/bid/14416/100-Awesome-Marketing-Stats-Charts-Graphs-Data.aspx

If you are spending money for marketing companies and do not know what they are doing or seeing meaningful results, you might be throwing money out the window. The market has shifted and continues to shift away from traditional marketing and SEO, and toward reputation marketing that connects with people who are looking for a dentist, *when* they are looking for a dentist, and *where* they are looking for a dentist. The best bang for your buck in this Google age is a combination of video marketing, reputation marketing, and targeted keyword campaigns if you want to promote something specific like dental implants or Invisalign.

You have such an amazing opportunity here to be in front of those people who are looking for the services that you are offering. Let's take advantage of it.

For a fraction of the money many dentists throw away by hiring marketing companies without seeing any meaningful results or knowing what they are doing, you can implement and even automate a reputation marketing campaign that builds value over time and sends you a steady stream of new patients each and every month.

Two words of warning before we prepare to implement your reputation marketing plan.

First, reputation marketing is not a get-rich-quick scheme. A good reputation marketing plan takes a few months to start gaining momentum and up to a year or so to reach its full potential for your practice. But it is the most effective way to consistently attracts new patients to your practice in a way you can control, and does not cost you thousands of dollars a month. It's worth it.

Second, before you move on, remember, education without implementation is just entertainment. I do not want to just entertain you here. I want to help you succeed. That can only happen if you implement the plan I will share with you here. When I speak around the country, I follow up with offices a few months later, and they have not implemented a single thing they learned from the seminar. We call that procrastination, and unfortunately dentists are known to be the kings of doing that. Don't fall into this category. Let's get started. Let me help you get more credible and more visible online with Step One: Getting Found.

Part 1

Getting Found Online

CHAPTER 1

Laying the Foundation

I t does not matter how great your dental practice is; it will not do anybody any good if nobody knows you exist. Decades ago, getting found involved direct mail, full-page ads in the Yellow Pages, and community marketing campaigns. Once people learned of you, they would then ask family or friends if they knew you, confirm with their insurance plan if you were in-network, and then decide whether to visit. Or, a patient might simply ask someone for a recommendation of a good dentist.

Today, that is not good enough. That is no longer the process most people use to choose a dentist. There may be a place for very targeted direct-mail campaigns, such as with sending a promotion to current or former patients. Community marketing can help you connect with local residents and give back to your community. Phone book advertising is useful in very limited circumstances, such as with older or rural populations. But those types of promotions are flawed for many reasons. Traditional marketing is like the dinosaur or the dodo bird—it is extinct.

Breaking Away from Ineffective Tactics

The biggest problem with traditional tactics for getting found is they do not reflect how people *actually look* for dentists today. In other words, even if they work to get people to notice you, they will not help you much because they fail to put you in front of people looking for a dentist. People do not look for dentists in their mailbox, the phone book, or community events. They look online by using short search terms such as "best dentist" and their city or town.

A 2018 HubSpot study shows that 50% of online searches have only three words. "Best dentist, Chicago" fits right into that research. Remember, word-of-mouth is now "word-of-*mouse*." Patients are reading what others are saying about you online and making decisions based on those comments. I call this new transition to Word of Mouth 2.0, and it has become the backbone to the new patient flow for most practices. A good 35 to 45% of your new patients should come from existing patients who tell others about your services.

So, if your marketing targets their mailboxes instead of their internet search results, you are unlikely to catch their attention when they are thinking about choosing a dentist. Even if they see your ad, they will not pay much attention. Ranking high in online search results for terms like "best dentist" or "dentist" plus your city, town, or other geographic location positions you in front of people at the exact time they are looking for a dentist in your area. Thus, if your marketing pushes you up in the search results, almost everyone who sees you is getting ready to choose a dentist.

The moment right before someone makes a decision to purchase something online has been termed by Google the Zero Moment of Truth (ZMOT). Google research reveals that 88% of U.S. consumers now engage in ZMOT before making their decision.[4] It refers to the point in the buying cycle when the patient researches a service, often before the office even knows that they exist. (Note that when a patient of yours refers a friend or family member, it may not be the right time for that person to call you. Referrals will typically call when they are due for re-care or have a dental emergency—that's when ZMOT occurs for those people. They generally won't research you or make a decision about choosing a dentist until one of those situations arise.) You can read more about ZMOT at ThinkWithGoogle.com

---

INDUSTRY INSIGHTS

Thanks to how quickly we can discover information, your customers often know exactly what they want before they visit you.

Before the internet and mobile devices, your customers discovered your business pretty simply. First, an initial stimulus would catch the attention of your customer—something like a radio ad, television spot, or a spot in the phone book for your business. Next, if this sparked their interest, they'd immediately head to your business. They'd buy the product or service they were interested in, and experience the "First Moment of Truth." Then, afterward, they see if expectations match reality. Did they love their experience? Hate whatever it is they bought?

Often, consumers share bad experiences with friends and family; that's important to keep in mind, especially because of how things have changed. Now, people research your business before they enter your front door! The moment people are making decisions is happening *online*. Google calls this the

---

4   https://www.thinkwithgoogle.com/consumer-insights/the-zero-moment-of-truth-macro-study/

"Zero Moment of Truth," and it's happening every single day for your business.

Since 88% of all buying decisions are made online at the Zero Moment of Truth, businesses need to understand how their marketing is performing exactly at that point.

—Evan Lazarus, *Simple Impact Media*

What influences ZMOT? According to Moz.com, one of the preeminent search engine research companies, your local citations and online reviews are two of the most important (and controllable) things that go into getting found online. Of course, the point is not to just get found. It is to get found by the right people (i.e., people searching for a dentist), in the right place (i.e., *where* they go to find a dentist), at the right time (i.e., *when* they are looking for a dentist).

I will show you how to use listings, also known as *local citations*, and online reviews to help you do that without adding a bunch of more work to your day. I will also point out why citations are a very important signal in local map search rankings. Have you ever done a local search and noticed another dentist with fewer reviews ranking higher than you in the local map pack? Most likely, this office has more consistent citations than your office.

Tip: When you do a search on Google or any search other engine, remember to use the Incognito or private browsing mode. Why? Many times, offices have told me that they rank in a certain position—but they've been searching on a device they have searched on before. Google remembers the search history, which throws off the results. If you use Incognito or private browsing mode, you get the results that your patients will probably see when they are searching for you.

Another site with some great local data is LocalFalcon.com, which allows you to look at any search term and see how your office ranks on the map pack of Google. It will probably open your eyes and show you how good or bad your local SEO is. I was recently talking with a dentist in Westchester, New York, who claimed his well-known marketing company was doing an amazing job generating new patients. However, when we looked at how he was ranking under some local SEO terms such as "dentist near me," "dentist [town]," etc., he realized that even when he was standing in front of his own office (the program displays real-time results), he was not even number one. Once the searcher moved slightly from his office location, this dentist was ranked 10 or below, and in some places 20 or below. It was an eye-opening experience for him to realize that a company he was paying had so completely dropped the ball. I share this story with you because I don't want to see it happen to fellow dentists.

Here is a screenshot of my office under Invisalign…

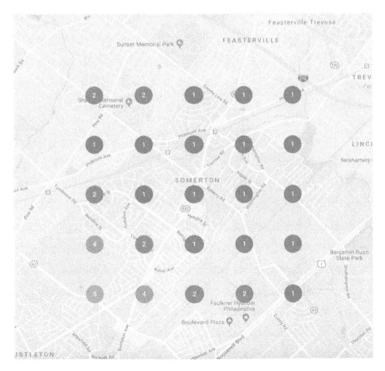

Now take a look and see what this office I described above looks like.

You can clearly see how poorly this office is ranking on the map section of Google.

Another problem with traditional tactics for getting found is that people do not go straight from finding a dentist to making an appointment. After learning about a dentist, many people search the internet for the dentist's or practice's name to look at reviews or social media postings about them before making an appointment. A 2019 study from Software Advice shows that 94% of patients use online reviews to evaluate physicians—up from 82% in 2018.

Thus, even if a traditional tactic reaches the right people at the right time, they are going to search for you online before deciding whether to make an appointment with you. I can see it firsthand. As a general dentist who does a lot of restorative dentistry, I am constantly referring my patients to specialists such as an endodontist for root canal therapy, and an oral surgeon for implant placement. In the past, most patients would take the referral card from me and immediately call the office to schedule an appointment. Now, however, they take out their mobile phones and look up the office online before making the decision to make an appointment. This is a great example of how important social proof is for a dental office—even if they are a word of mouth practice, as many specialists are.

In these circumstances, people generally search for both the dentist's name and the practice name along with word like "reviews," "insurance," or "costs" to see what others are saying about the dentist online and how much it would cost to have that person as their dentist. If they don't find anything, or if they find a bunch of negative information, they move on to the next dentist, often by conducting a search like the one I mentioned with the first problem, some variation of "best dentist in [their city or town]." Are you putting your best effort forward? Where are your reviews found? Are they on the sites that matter or elsewhere?

A Better and More Effective Way to Get Found Online

With most people searching for you online before making an appointment, it is more important than ever to establish an online presence that matches how people look for dentists today. That means your online presence must do two things.

First, your online presence must push your practice to the **top of the search results** when people look for dentists in your area. This requires you to invest your time and energy making sure you will appear in front of the right people (i.e., people searching for a dentist), in the right place (i.e., where they go to find a dentist), at the right time (i.e., when they are looking for a dentist). This is the visibility I was discussing earlier.

Second, your online presence must build **trust** with people who search for you before making an appointment, so when people search for you, they see lots of positive information that is proven to compel people to trust you and make an appointment with you. As BrightLocal reveals, 68% of consumers say that are more likely to trust a business with positive reviews.

You need both of these: top search results and trust. You can't have one without the other. Please don't confuse them. Being visible without being credible is a problem, because people won't come in since you don't have reviews. And being credible without being visible is a problem as nobody is going to be seeing the reviews in the first place.

Now we'll focus on helping you lay the foundation for getting found online by the right people, in the right place, and at the right time by highlighting two simple actions you can take to build searchability and credibility, plus a third that might surprise you.

A Different Type of Search Engine Optimization

Getting found online as part of a reputation marketing plan is a slightly different concept than what most people refer to as search engine optimization, or SEO. In basic terms, SEO is how practices improve their odds of appearing high on the search results. Although a number of factors go into that calculation, two stand out as the most effective and controllable ways to get found when people search for a dentist.

With dental practices, people frequently search using a location element, such as "best dentist near me" or "best dentist in Philadelphia." When they do, Google's search results will include a map showing three or four dentists (the fourth is usually a paid advertisement) in the location that an algorithm calculates most likely to interest them. Below the map, Google will include additional organic search results, including authoritative websites listing a number of dentists and a few specific practice websites, and some results from practices that pay Google to show them on the front page. (Just so you know, physical location may play a role in rankings.)

INDUSTRY INSIGHTS

Online reviews, particularly Google reviews, account for an estimated 15% of the SEO pie.[5]

This means Google reviews could prove critical for SEO in highly competitive markets, and may be all you need in markets that have lower competition.

While online reviews may not prove necessary for SEO purposes, conversion rate optimization is where reviews give you the most mileage. The journey from online searcher, to new patients in your practice, to case acceptance of operative care, may involve looking at your reviews. There's a natural instinct to look for negative reviews to see if others had any "buyer's remorse," so to speak. Every busy practice will eventually get some negative reviews.

This is why it's critical to continually earn positive, glowing 5-star reviews on a regular basis. Such new reviews will also naturally contain SEO "keywords." Keywords are things that people search for in order to find a dentist in your area. When online reviews have keywords such as your city name, "dentist," or the name of specific dental procedures, these keywords in your patient's reviews help you get found.

As tempting as it is, you should never pay for a review. It is against Google's terms of conditions.[6] If they catch you, they can deactivate your business page.

---

5   https://moz.com/local-search-ranking-factors
6   https://blog.reviews.io/thinking-of-buying-google-reviews-think-again

Depending on your specific market, online reviews may fully or partially alleviate ongoing SEO fees. They help patients choose you over other dentists in your area who have fewer reviews. They provide insight on areas of improvement in your practice. And they can help you actually improve the ROI from your SEO efforts, by improving conversions.

—Justin Morgan, *SEO specialist*

With all the competition from authoritative listing websites, the easiest way to improve your odds of appearing on the first page of Google's search results is to first attempt to become one of the three or four practices on the map results. Getting featured on the map is much easier than earning one of the organic search results because you do not have to compete against highly authoritative sites such as Yelp!, YellowPages.com, Healthgrades, Zocdoc, RateMDs, Vitals, and Angie's List. Additionally, getting on the map does not require you to pay Google anything. With paid placement, you need to continue to pay Google if you want to continue to appear on the first page. When you stop paying, your phone stops ringing. That is not the case with the map.

Finally, the two things you can do to help you get on the map results will also help you get found in a compelling way. Not only will you appear on more Google search results over time, but you also will show up in a way that makes people want to make an appointment with you.

Specifically, the first way to improve your search rankings is to make sure your practice is accurately listed on the websites search engines look to when deciding which dentists to include in their search results. In the online search world, this is called optimizing your local citations. By optimizing your local citations, you will create a large consistent footprint online. As simple as this sounds, listings websites often have inaccurate or incomplete information. I will walk you through how to optimize your local citations manually or in an automated fashion later in the book.

The second way to improve your search rankings is to regularly collect online reviews from your patients, focusing especially on Google reviews. In fact, Google recently downgraded the value of reviews from other sites such as Facebook and Demandforce reviews, treating them only as "votes" on Google instead of real reviews. Facebook does not even collect reviews anymore; they are now called "recommendations." Patients no longer have the option to rate you on a star rating scale of 1 to 5. Instead, they answer a simple question: "Do you recommend (business name)? Yes or No?" (More on this later.) Google has always been the safest and best way to go simply because it controls the internet.

With a couple dozen Google reviews and optimized local citations, your practice will start to get noticed by Google, especially in suburban and rural areas, where you are not competing with hundreds of practices. In urban areas, continued efforts will still help you; it will just take longer for them to help you stand out because there are more dentists vying for attention. I like to say the gold standard for Google reviews is 100. When you hit that number, you really stand out online. But the sky's the limit; don't stop gathering reviews just because you think you have enough. You never have enough if you want to continue to remain relevant to both Google and those who trust online reviews. I have seen practices that collect reviews at a nice fast clip and then they stop generating them as their attention shifts to other details within the daily operations of running a dental practice. Guess what happens to their map rankings? They drop.

BrightLocal indicated in the 2019 Local Consumer Review Survey that the "star rating" and "number of reviews" are number one and two factors that consumers use to assess a local business. This makes sense, as the patients clearly see very quickly your total number of reviews and a star rating when doing a Google search. It takes searches only a couple of seconds to make a decision whether you are a trusted business or to look elsewhere. Only 13% of consumers will give a business with 1 or 2 stars a chance.

How Reviews Impact Consumer Behavior:

Consumers read an average of 10 reviews before feeling able to trust a local business.

- The average local business has 39 reviews on Google My Business.
- 57% of consumers only use businesses with four or more review stars.
- Improving your review star rating by 1.5 could lead to 13,000 more leads.

—BrightLocal 2019 Local Consumer Review Study[7]

When I was in grade school, I learned the fundamental three "Rs—reading, 'riting and 'rithmatic. In the online review space, the three Rs also form the foundation of your online presence: Regularity, Recent Reviews, and Ratings. (Some people say there are actually 5 Rs: Patient Recommendation, Reviews' Recency, Your Responses, and Retention). However you look at it, mastering these principles is so important to becoming the go-to dentist in your town.

Before we move to the next section on claiming and optimizing your local citations, here are my perspectives on the three Rs for the online review space.

---

7   https://www.brightlocal.com/resources/online-reviews-statistics-2019/

Regularity

Google has alerted everyone that stagnant websites not upgraded frequently can drop in search rankings compared to those websites that are updated often with content, blog posts, articles, etc. Reviews provide your practice with a source of user-created content that if you handle online reputation properly you should have them coming in on a regular basis. Google has even picked some of the reviews and added them to Google My Business knowledge panels for everyone searching to see. Google will determine which reviews are most relevant and will show those first as they are more trusted.

Just having a star rating is no longer enough. Reviews work, as long as they are not only added frequently but are also authentic. As BrightLocal found in its 2019 Local Consumer Study, most people say that they need to read at least 10 opinions before making a final decision. If you have fewer than 10 reviews, there is a good chance that the searcher will pass you buy and choose a business they trust more, so if you have more feedback than your competition, you are already a step ahead. The gold standard is 100 reviews, but it's also very location specific. To be relevant, you want to have the most reviews, or to at least be close. For example, if a competitor has 300 reviews on Google, that should be the number you target.

On a side note, we are going to be discussing how to generate reviews consistent from your happy patients in a few pages, but that is the key—*you need happy patients who receive consistent high quality of care.* If there are issues in your office, believe me, the reviews will tell the story. Patients also like to share positive experiences with others, and they just may not know the way to go about doing it in a way that helps you online. This is where your team plays a major role. Help your team understand the importance of reviews and help them tell patients that their reviews matter and contribute to your success online and in the office.

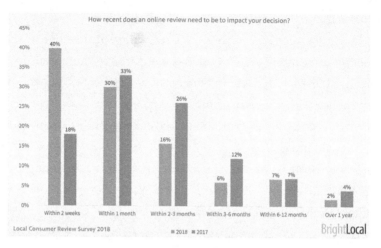

Image Credit: BrightLocal

Recency

What is truly amazing looking at the above data from a statistical standpoint is the fact that 40% of consumers want to see reviews from the last two weeks and 85% of people think reviews older than three months are irrelevant. In addition, look at the change from 2017 to 2018. In a single year, the number of consumers who want reviews from within two weeks went up from 18% to 40%. That is a huge change from one year to the next. Patients want to know what others are saying about the current state of your practice—not what was going on last year when there may have been staff turnover, etc. You need to be up to the minute with fresh content, and this applies to reviews as well. You should be constantly encouraging reviews.

Recent reviews are usually the first to appear when searchers click through to read them on Google, Yelp!, etc. These sites also give the user an option to sort reviews by highest, lowest, newest, and most relevant. If a prospective patient has seen a lot of recent reviews from your patients, it shows them that you are currently providing great care, and it will help them make that decision to become your patient so much easier.

Ratings

As we have seen, results with the best ratings and the most reviews tend to be at the top of Google searches. Practices listed on page one are most likely to be seen and clicked on, especially if those practices have reviews. This visibility draws new patients to your practice and many times these patients already trust you based on what others have written. On the flip side, a low star rating will often discourage people from clicking through—or those low ratings can even push you further down the list.

When people are searching for a dentist (without recommendations), star ratings and number of reviews are the quickest way for them to determine an opinion. Even having one less star or significantly less reviews for your practice could send potential new patients to your competition. Having no ratings could mean that the searcher thinks you are a either a new business, or they may wonder why nobody has provided feedback about your office before. It raises a lot of red flags, and the searcher may second-guess becoming your patient. Your goal should be to make the best first impression and present the best possible image of your practice to those searching.

Many of your patients are using mobile devices to find a dentist, so the reviews are even closer than you ever expected them to be. They are in the palm of their hands. You also know that to be the most successful online you need to have good SEO practices into place for your website—but major review websites often have greater visibility in search results. You need to know which sites have the most influence on search results and thus where to focus your online reputation attention.

What follows is a quick view list with descriptions of the most important sites—monitor and make sure you get reviews on them. (Please note: This is a list as of 2019; at any time the list is subject to change, and in the internet world, I guarantee it will. For recent updates, please go to DrLenTau.com and subscribe to my blog.)

Review Sites Most Important to Your Success

According to BrightLocal, the majority of consumers look at multiple review sites before making a decision about a business. Specifically, according to their data, 20% of consumers look at one review site, 59% look at two or three sites, 16% look at four or five review sites, and 5% look at six or more review sites. Thus, it's critical to build a broad footprint across multiple review sites, including general review sites and ones specific to healthcare.

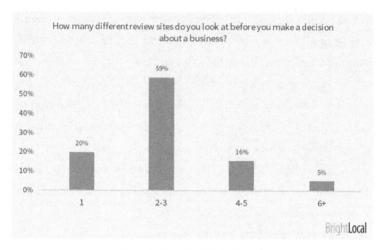

Image Credit: BrightLocal

General Review Sites

According to BrightLocal's Local Consumer Review Survey, in 2018, consumers read an average of ten reviews before they can trust a business. That number was up from 7 in 2017.

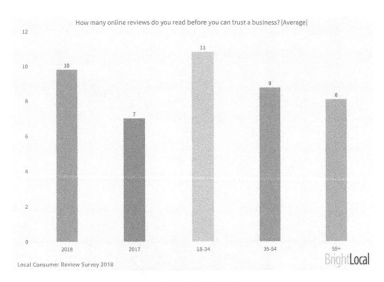

Image Credit: BrightLocal

As you can see, the younger the consumer, the more reviews they read before trusting a company. Consumers who are 18–34 years old lead the way, reading an average of 11 reviews, followed by 35–54-year-olds, who read an average of nine, and those who are 55+ reading an average of eight. We expect this trend to continue to increase as more people look for reviews to help them choose dentists.

Because many consumers will not know to look at review sites that are specific to healthcare, instead just searching Google, it's important to make sure your online presence includes reviews at the most important general review sites as well as healthcare-specific sites. Here are the most important general review sites to focus on.

Google

As of this writing, Google accounts for 88.1% of search-engine market share. According to a ReviewTrackers 2018 survey, meanwhile, **Google is the review site of choice:** 63.6% of consumers say they are likely to check online reviews on Google before visiting a business—more than any other review site.[8]

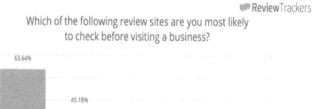

Image Credit: ReviewTrackers

Consider also these statistics from Internet Live Stats, Statista and Blue Corona:

- 3.5 billion Google searches are made every day.
- The volume of Google searches grows by roughly 10% every year.
- Every year, somewhere between 16% and 20% of Google searches are new—they've never been searched before.
- 90% of desktop searches are done via Google.
- 60% of Google searches are done via mobile devices. Only five years ago, the figure was nearly half that—34%.
- Google captures 95% of the mobile search engine market in the U.S.

---

8   https://www.reviewtrackers.com/reports/online-reviews-survey/

- Roughly a third of all mobile Google searches are related to location.

Meanwhile, BrightLocal's Google Reviews Study of 13,341 dentists (found using 1,799 related keywords) reveals that:
- 84% of dentists have Google reviews.
- Dentists have an average of 38 Google reviews.
- On average, dentists have 4.6 stars.

Clearly, Google reviews are essential. You must get these reviews to not only rank higher on the local map pack, but also to be relevant. For those in California who think Yelp! is all that you need, think again. Dominate Google, dominate search ranking … repeat that three times.

WHY PATIENTS DON'T LEAVE GOOGLE REVIEWS

If you have struggled to get patients to leave Google reviews, understanding why patients don't leave reviews is a great first step to start getting some. I have personally surveyed more than 1,000 patients to better understand why they do and don't leave their dentist a Google review. Here are the most popular answers I was given:
- They forget.
- They forget their Google password.
- It takes too long.
- "Out of sight out of mind."
- They're too busy.
- They don't know what to write.
- They don't know how to leave a review.
- It takes too many steps.

The top reasons are the top two, that they forget to leave a review or forget their Google password. This makes the steps I share later in the book even more important. Those are designed to send gentle reminders to patients and make leaving Google reviews *very* easy.

Yelp!

The moment when people looking for a business on Yelp! is at a critical point when they are ready to make a buying decision. When people are reading Yelp! reviews they are usually on the verge of becoming patients, and a couple of positive reviews could be enough to get them into your office. Patients are encouraged to write longer reviews and they normally do, sometimes with very detailed accounts of their experiences in their office.

In general, reviews on Yelp! are longer than reviews on Google. Just like on your Google My Business page, with a Yelp! business listing, you can add your own content so that you have more control over the way your business is presented. Yelp! customers can add their own photos along with their reviews, but they may not always be the best images. Adding your own photos to the business listing can be a good way to tailor your brand image and make your Yelp! page look more appealing.

Yelp! is useful for website rankings and getting your business seen online. In SEO terms, Yelp! is considered an "authority" site, meaning that it can carry more weight and help boost traffic to your site. According to a 2018 study by ReviewTrackers, 45% of customers say they are likely to check Yelp! reviews before visiting a business, a percentage second only to Google. If you claim your Yelp! listing, you can add a link directly to your website, and it will boost your rankings in Google.

Facebook

Facebook isn't always the first place business owners think of when it comes to online reviews, but Facebook reviews are becoming increasingly important. No matter what demographics you're trying to reach, a significant chunk of your dream audience is on Facebook, where they're sharing recommendations with friends and perusing reviews written by strangers.

According to a 2019 study by RevLocal, about half of consumers check Facebook reviews for small businesses, and 80% of consumers are likely to choose a business with positive Facebook feedback. Ratings appear on the main menu, providing an instant snapshot of the way your patients feel about your practice. Searching for your business on Facebook also shows how many "likes" you have (another form of social proof).

Healthcare Review Sites

Some sites focus specifically on healthcare providers to give patients a way to find doctors in any field. The reviews may carry a lot of weight and are likely to appear high in search results depending on your overall internet presence.

Healthgrades

Healthgrades is an online database of doctors, dentists, and hospitals that has more than 100 million users and has amassed data on more than three million U.S. healthcare providers. The site gets an average of 7.6 million visits in the U.S. every month.

When a patient searches Google for your practice, Healthgrades will likely show up on the first page. To be very upfront and honest about my opinion of Healthgrades, I have never gotten a patient from Healthgrades or have even been told by a caller that they found my office on Healthgrades. A few companies well known in the dental space (Sesame, Solution Reach, and doctor.com) have special relationships with Healthgrades and will make it seem like Healthgrades is super important to your success. I tell you to use some caution in deciding if you want to use Healthgrades in your dental office.

Rate MDs

Rate MDs is much more popular and important in Canada than it is in the U.S. It has more than 1.7 million providers and 2.6 million doctor reviews, and its tagline is Doctors You Can Trust. According to the website, more than 100 million potential patients use RateMDs for information before making important health care decisions. RateMDs allows patients to rate physicians as well as their staff, punctuality, helpfulness, and knowledge. Patients are also able to leave personal comments about their experience, and they can do this anonymously.

When patients search for a physician by area, they will be provided with the 200 top-ranked physicians in that region. In order to get closer to the top, physicians need more reviews that have higher rankings. If you can prove a fraudulent review was posted, RateMDs will take the review down. RateMDs also adds awards to profiles when they repeatedly receive good reviews.

Vitals

Similar to Healthgrades and RateMDs, Vitals is an online database of medical professionals where patients can search for healthcare options based on specialty, doctor, or condition. The average number of monthly U.S. visits is 4.2 million. Filters can be applied for accepted insurance and location. Vitals states that its goal is to connect people with the "best medical care" in their areas.

Vitals also has advertising on its site. These ads may confuse patients and lure them away from your practice listings. In my opinion, this site is more important if you are a physician rather than a dentist. Vitals will likely show up on the first page of a Google search, which can have a negative effect if you have a low rating. While Vitals filters excessively negative reviews with no true standing, the anonymity granted to patients can sometimes be abused.

Zocdoc

Zocdoc is a popular online appointment scheduling system that is widely used across the healthcare industry. Patients use the platform to discover doctors in their area, read other patient reviews, and to schedule appointments. Since launching in 2007, Zocdoc has become a household name in the healthcare industry and now has an average of 3.8 million monthly U.S. visits. Its innovative platform provides patients with a modern way to search for in-network doctors by insurance provider, book appointments outside of business hours, and read patient reviews, all in one place.

Today, many dentists pay a $300 monthly fee to list their practice on Zocdoc, but this is changing in some markets. To help solicit more patient reviews for you, Zocdoc will email the patient after their appointment has ended, asking, "How was your appointment with Dr. ___?" The next time they sign into Zocdoc, patients will also see a pop-up notification asking them to leave a review.

These reviews show up in your Zocdoc Profile results on search engine results pages (SERPs), but because they don't end up on Google, their effects are somewhat limited other than to Zocdoc users. Please note that only Zocdoc patients can review your office.

Care Dash

You may not have heard of CareDash, but you probably will soon. The newest site to the list claims to be one of the most transparent healthcare review platforms for doctors. It had 1 million searches in March 2019 alone. The platform allows patients to look for doctors and dentists in their area and compare ratings of different providers so that they can choose the best one. Patients can also share their experience by leaving a review and rating.

Meanwhile, healthcare providers and practice managers can claim and manage doctor profiles for free. They can also respond to patients' reviews and improve overall engagement. CareDash also has a library of information with tips and advice to help both patients and doctors.

Dentistry.com

Dentistry.com, like the other sites listed, has a robust amount of dental reviews, and an average of nearly 1 million visits per month in the U.S. What distinguishes this site from the rest is its community feature, where real dentists answer community members' dental questions.

Its "Expert Corner" features helpful articles written by dentists. And Dentistry.com also features a booking tool.

What's Next?

The best way to take advantage of this information is to determine which sites are the best for your presence. But it's not enough to simply set up a profile and sit back and wait for the reviews to come in. Patients won't take the time to provide reviews without being prompted in one way or another.

In the next chapter, I will show you two ways to claim and optimize your local citations. I will then provide more information on online reviews and how implementing a simple online review marketing plan like the one in Chapter 6 not only makes people want to come to you as their dentist but will also simultaneously help improve your search rankings.

CHAPTER 2

Claiming and Optimizing Your Local Citations

Before you start reading this section, open up an internet browser and go to Yext.com. You will enter whether you are a single location or have multiple locations, and your business name and phone number. Enter the information from your Google My Business listing. What is the score that is reported back? Just so you understand, you want your score to be as close to 100% as possible. The closer to 100 percent, the more consistent your listings or local citations are. The closer to 0 percent, the more errors or inconsistencies you will see in your local citations. Disregard the last column if it says not verified through Yext; the other information is important.

Local citations, like the term suggests, are the mentions of—or citations to—your practice on other websites.

The most well-known listing websites are Yelp!, Zocdoc, YellowPages. com, and Healthgrades, but more than 120 relevant websites list dental practices including Google, Factual, Facebook, RateMDs, Vitals, and more.

Your local citations include three parts: your name, your address, and your phone number, also referred to by the acronym NAP. Some sites will include additional information such as your website, reviews, hours of operation, scheduling capabilities, or insurance information. So you may actually see it now referred to as NAPW (name, address, phone number and website). Additionally, some like Yelp!, Google, and YellowPages.com are general in nature and do not focus on a specific industry. Others, like Zocdoc and Healthgrades, are industry specific.

Reviews and listings in your local citations are a big part of getting onto map search results, as this graphic shows.

Local Pack/Finder Ranking Factors

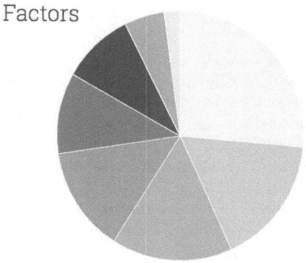

1. **Google My Business Signals** (Proximity, categories, keyword in business title, etc.) **25.12%**

2. **Link Signals** (Inbound anchor text, linking domain authority, linking domain quantity, etc.) **16.53%**

3. **Review Signals** (Review quantity, review velocity, review diversity, etc.) **15.44%**

4. **On-Page Signals** (Presence of NAP, keywords in titles, domain authority, etc.) **13.82%**

5. **Citation Signals** (IYP/aggregator NAP consistency, citation volume, etc.) **10.82%**

Your practice is already listed on dozens of websites even if you don't submit your information, but unless you are optimizing your listings, your local citations could be harming your practice.

For example, when I purchased my practice, the Pennsylvania Center for Dental Excellence back in 2007, the previous doctor's name appeared on many local directories. But many years earlier, the practice was called Daisy Dental Care, and that name was still floating around online, confusing the most important site of them all: Google.

The good news is you can optimize them easily either on your own or with some help, which can help your online reputation and two key ways: search rankings and reputation protection. It will also help you gain an important key with Google: trust.

The Impact of Local Citations on Your Practice's Search Rankings

Your citations have the ability to push you up local search results if they are done right or bury you if they are not. This is because one of the trust factors search engines consider when deciding which dentists to list first is how many times your practice is mentioned online correctly.

For example, in July 2014, Google updated its algorithm (called Pigeon) in an attempt to become more location-specific, provide more relevant and accurate local search results. Google did so by focusing results on a relevant "centroid," or a central point of relevance. The first centroid Google used to return more relevant local results was the center of the city or town searched.

During that time, dental practices near a city center tended to be ranked higher up the search results when someone searched for "dentist" or "best dentist" plus a city or town. This update had a dramatic effect on my office as before this update, I was always ranking on the map section of Google during a search for a dentist in Philadelphia. My office is about 25 miles from center city Philadelphia, so when this update hit, my local map ranking for Philadelphia searches took a dramatic hit.

A few years later, Google shifted to an industry-centered approach. During that time, Google considered the densest cluster of businesses in an industry as the central point of relevance and prioritizing businesses near that cluster as the most relevant.

Today, Google uses a user-centered approach, prioritizing results close to the physical location of the user, even when someone searches for "dentists in [my town]." This shift is even more pronounced noticeable in mid-to-large cities with many neighborhoods or districts and a competitive business environment.

If your practice is listed on many sites correctly, search engines will consider it important. If not, they consider it less important. Additionally, when people search for local businesses—as they do for dentists—many search engines highlight a few local practices on a map at the top of the search results, even before they give organic search results.

Google, for example, organically includes three local practices on a map right below the sponsored ads and above the local results (called the map pack, snack pack, or the 3-pack). Landing in the map pack pays back big time. Research shows that for local search rankings:

Position 1 gets nearly 24.46% of all clicks.

Position 2 gets 13.38% of all clicks.

Position 3 gets 10.12% of all clicks.

…and local listings after the 6th-ranking position each get less than 2% of the clicks. (So if you're after the 6th position, you might as well not exist.)

Citations are one of the most important factors that impact the map search results, so having your practice listed on several trustworthy websites can give you a better chance of appearing on the first page of search results—in the map section—even if you do not yet appear on the first page of the organic search results. Now, do a local search in an Incognito browser for a dentist and your town. How do you show up? Or, I should ask, *where* do you show up? Are you on the map in the top three? If you are, great. If not, you have work to do, and I'll keep helping you.

A Word of Caution

When your citations are not optimized, they can bury you. Search engines will not reconcile even the slightest inconsistencies and will consider each listing a different business. That means having information listed inconsistently across different listing sites can hurt your search engine rankings. To put this in simpler terms, you are basically being penalized if your information is not consistent. Continuing to ignore this can and will be detrimental to your practice.

Even worse, if one citation is wrong or inconsistent, the inconsistency will come up over and over again on other sites because they all pull data from each other, and they all talk to search engines such as Google.

Image Credit Whitespark, Inc. and Tidings Company LLC

With my practice, I had another citation come up with a different practice name. As I mentioned, my practice name is Pennsylvania Center for Dental Excellence. The listing has it as Pennsylvania Center-Dental. I have no idea where that name came from, but once it got out there, it started coming up everywhere. When we found it, we changed it, but it is important to pay attention to such inconsistencies. This is something that is very difficult to manage manually, constantly checking the information online to make sure it is correct. We then had another name we used online, Pennsylvania Center for Dental Excellence: Leonard F. Tau DMD PC. As you can tell this name is very long—in fact, too long for many of the local directories, so we soon dropped my name and decided on Pennsylvania Center for Dental Excellence.

If your information is inconsistent, search engines view that as a sign your online presence is untrustworthy and think your practice is either disorganized, or even out of business, pushing you far down their search results. Because many sites pull information from others, if your information is wrong on one site, it is likely wrong on others, too.

The analogy I use it is like giving someone a business card with the wrong information on it. That is something you would never want to do, so why would you want it happening where everyone is looking for a dentist?

Do not worry. The rest of this chapter will walk you through exactly what to do to get your citations working for you to help you get found online.

Primary Data Aggregators

Have you ever wondered how business data gets distributed across the web? Or why local businesses sometimes appear in directories without ever having submitted a listing themselves? It all comes down to data aggregators. Data aggregators are data mining systems that spread business information online. They collect and share business data with a multitude of sources, including search engines like Google.

Data aggregators are responsible for transmitting much of the data that exists in the local search ecosystem. They propagate a business' information to a variety of publishing outlets, including search engines, social media platforms, review sites, and business directories.

Although data aggregators are very good at spreading data around, they can't differentiate between accurate and outdated information. So it's up to local businesses to ensure aggregators have accurate listing data, including the name, address, and phone number (NAP) of each business location.

Otherwise, the business will face a series of problems caused by bad data, including duplicate listings, inconsistent NAP, and inaccurate local citations. Plus, having a disjointed local presence hurts the business' reputation among search engines and consumers.

In the U.S. four major players disseminate business data online: Infogroup, Neustar/Localeze, Factual, and Foursquare. These companies collect local business information and have massive data-sets in which they validate and vet the information provided. Search engines such as Google, Bing, and Apple license the primary aggregators' data. Other sites including Facebook, Yelp!, Yellowpages, CityGrid, and Dun & Bradstreet also play a role in sending data feeds to search engines.

Search engines manage their own databases, but the information comes from the aforementioned sources. If the business data on any of these primary sources is incorrect, it can override the information that is already available in the search engines' databases, and this can lead to either new listings being created or changing existing listing data. Bad NAP can negatively impact your ability to rank on Google and other sites.

THE BOTTOM LINE:
DENTISTS NEED TO TAKE CONTROL OF THEIR DATA.
Monitoring business citations for inaccuracies and submitting accurate details to aggregators is one of the most important ways local businesses can keep their data clean.

Your citations impact how easy it is to find negative information about your practice.

Because search engines view many of the listing websites such as Yelp! and YellowPages.com as trustworthy, they will often include your practice's listing among the first organic search results. That means your reviews on those high-trust listing sites will be somewhat easy to find.

Thus, optimizing your citations makes the strategies I show you in Parts 2 and 3 even more important and impactful for your practice.

In addition, creating a larger positive online presence by optimizing your listings on the most important websites makes it harder for negative information on lower-trust sites to find their way onto the first page of search results.

If you are listed on 100 sites that search engines see as trustworthy, it is likely that a negative blog post by a disgruntled patient will be pushed off the first page of Google's search results. Without that strong online footprint, negative information has a much better chance of making it to the front page. Then, it takes on a life of its own because when people click on a link in response to a search—which is likely to happen when something negative makes its way to the first page—this tells search engines that link is relevant. It's a vicious cycle.

Let's take a step back and talk about your online presence for a few minutes. I want you to do a Google search for the name of your business right now. The first thing you should see is your business on the right side of the page. (This is a relatively new feature , which I will discuss more in an upcoming section.) If not, that is a problem. On the left side, what does the first page of the search engine results pages (SERPs) look like? Do you have your website listed multiple times, such as your homepage, "about us," "meet the doctor" and another internal page? After those, you may find your Yelp! page and Facebook and possibly sites such as CareCredit, Opencare, Indeed, etc. If this is what you look like, I am concerned with your overall online presence. Do you happen to see another dental office listed in those search results, maybe in another state or even around the corner with a similar name? That is another issue altogether.

The ideal first SERP page looks like the one below: your website is listed only once at the top, and then you have Facebook, Yelp!, and a number of other review sites with star ratings visible. Those star ratings being visible is key. An online review site without star ratings does not do you a whole lot of good. You may then have some YouTube videos that are showing now in the organic results, and finally you may find some social media sites if you are active in social media. This sets you up for long-term success and prevents malicious information from appearing on page one. The result gives you the best social proof for your practice.

What to Do with Local Citations to Get Found

Because search engines trust listing websites, the general rule is the more relevant places your business is cited correctly, the more search engines trust you and the higher you will rank on the search results. The problem is that a lot of these sites have wrong information, and if you are not diligent, the wrong information spawns like rabbits though these directories, affecting your local ranking.

Consider these factors affecting search results:

1. Are you a startup practice? If you have no online presence, you will need to get your information online in order to be found. This is super important, because if you worked somewhere else, that information comes up in searches for your name.

2. Did you recently buy a practice? Did you change the name of the practice? Make sure your name or the name of the practice is correct on all of these directories. I have seen firsthand how, eight to ten years after a dentist has bought a practice, directories still list old information.

3. Have you relocated your practice? If so, your address will most certainly be incorrect on these directories. Update the information so your patients know where you are located.

These are usually the most common issues office face, but there are others as well.

Getting your citations working for you requires only three steps:

1. You need to develop a content toolbox that includes exactly how you want your practice to appear on listing websites.

2. You need to decide what listing websites you want to make sure your information appears on.

3. You need to review and update your information on those sites so it will be recognized and trusted as you by search engines.

Here is everything you need to know and do for each of those steps.

Building Your Content Toolbox

The best and easiest way to optimize your local citation is to create a content toolbox. A content toolbox is a file or folder that has all your listing information in one place. This allows you to ensure all of your citations are complete and consistent and delegate or outsource the task of updating your citations with confidence.

Although updating citations is an important task, it is not one I suggest most dentists—especially busy dentists—do themselves. Rather, I suggest they learn how to do it and why it is important and then prepare a content toolbox they can provide to someone else to implement while they focus their time on other tasks only they can do.

The simplest way to do this is to have a folder on your computer or server dedicated to citations where you will keep relevant images, documents, and spreadsheets.

Although all citations will ask for your name, address, and phone number, which we refer to by the NAP acronym, many either request or allow you to include additional information, such as images, videos, a description of your business or services, business hours, coupons, and more.

In addition to ensuring your information is accurate, having a content toolbox allows you to delegate the task. Here is the information to include in your content toolbox.

NAP Contact Information

Decide exactly how you want your practice name to appear. If you are organized as a corporation, do you want to be listed as *Inc.* or *Incorporated*? If you are a limited liability company, do you want your name listed with a comma before the LLC reference? Do you want it to read *LLC, L.L.C.*, or *Limited Liability Company*?

Remove inconsistencies by picking one format and including it in your content toolbox. Speaking with thousands of dentists at my seminars, trade shows, and even over the phone, I've learned about so many issues when it comes to listed practice names. You want to make sure that the information online matches this listing. Here are some examples.

1. Dr. Leonard F. Tau DMD. Wrong—this is doctor, doctor—remove the Dr. prefix.

2. Dr. Leonard Tau. Wrong—this does not tell a searcher what type of doctor you are. You could be a gynecologist. Use DMD instead.

3. Leonard F. Tau DMD PC FAGD PHD FICOOI. *Way* too many titles at the end of your listing, and most people don't even know what these mean—leave it limited to DMD.

Your street address also needs to be consistent. For example, choose between Street, St., and Str. Choose between Ste. and Suite if you have a suite number. Confusion between *Ste.* and *Suite* is one of the biggest citation problems out there.

Finally, make sure your phone number on all listings is the same. Use a local number, not a toll-free number, and avoid using any tracking numbers. Tracking numbers are big problems with local citations. If you are using tracking numbers, they should never appear publicly because it will confuse search engines and hurt your SEO.[9]

9　Some very well-known companies use tracking numbers to track their results, but that number is the same on all sites, which tracks nothing since all the sites have the same information. The companies that do this need to prove their value to you and will tell you that they have generated so many leads. If someone has been referred to your practice, does a Google search, sees your Google My Business listing with a tracking number, and calls it, the company will claim they sent that patient to you. That could not be farther from the truth. Please be wary of these methods, and if you want a number to be listed, it should be your own.

For those looking for a call-tracking service, I personally use Patient Prism, which not only records your calls, and has unique phone numbers to track various marketing avenues, it also has coaches analyze the phone calls and grade the calls so your team can improve. I also recommend Call Tracker ROI, which Chris Phelps, a fellow dentist created. You can find out more about both of these companies on the resources sections of my website DrLenTau.com.

Make any tracking numbers invisible on the page because listing sites will pull it, and your local citations will become inconsistent. If it is appearing on your Google page, it means the number is visible, and it will screw up your search rankings. There are ways to hide your number from Google so you can still track your marketing efforts without making your citations inconsistent. If the companies providing your tracking numbers cannot or will not hide their number, you should consider dropping the tracking feature because the benefit of the call tracking can be vastly outweighed by the damage to your search rankings.

This happened to me, too. I was using a tracking number with a company that promised me they would keep it hidden but did not. My search rankings plummeted, and I ended up getting into a dispute with them over it.

Years later, they are still making up for it, and the tracking number still pops up in my local citations from time to time. If this happens to you, reputable companies will make up for it like the one I was using did with me. To find the latest list of companies I use or recommend to help you with this, visit the resources page at DrLenTau.com/BookResources.

Additional Information to Include in Your Toolbox

In addition to your NAP information, many listing sites allow you to include additional information, images, and videos. Adding this information helps you turn your local citations into even more powerful marketing tools because it adds more content for search engines to index, increases click throughs and conversions, and sets you apart from competitors in search results.

Here is additional information to include in your content toolbox to add to listing websites.

- Your website
- A contact email address
- A high-resolution company logo

- Photos of your office, team members, before-and-after transformations, and more
- Videos introducing yourself, answering frequently asked questions, touring your office, or of satisfied patients and happy team members
- Testimonials from happy patients
- Coupons or other offers for services you are looking to do more of
- Blog posts or other articles written by or about you and your practice
- Awards, seals, and accreditations received by you and your team

When anything changes, update your content toolbox and your local citations so they are all up to date. Additionally, if possible, include your address on every page on your website in the same way that matches your local citations. The footer is a good place to add your address to help your website get picked up by search engines that recognize the address.

Overcoming the Challenge of Multiple Office Locations

Practices with multiple office locations sometimes struggle with SEO because listing websites often get confused with all the different NAP information on their website to account for different addresses, phone numbers, and sometimes even slightly different practice names for each location, such as by including the city or neighborhood in the practice name. Thus, multilocation practices can end up buried in search results because different listing sites will pick up different information resulting in inconsistent local citations.

If you have multiple office locations, the first thing you should do is to avoid including NAP information for every office in one place. To do so, first, remove the NAP information in your footer. Instead, include a reference to "Our Locations" with clickable links that will open a new page with the full contact information for each location. Second, keep separate contact pages for each location instead of listing all addresses on one "contact us" page. You can do this by having a "contact us" dropdown menu with clickable links to each location under it. This will help you keep all offices separate for SEO purposes and avoid listing sites pulling different office addresses from the single "contact us" page.

Finally, set up separate local listings for each office on listing websites using the web address of the contact information page for that site. You could also create a simple, custom website for each location, otherwise known as location-specific microsites, where you include contact information for the microsite plus reviews, location-specific specials, hours, pictures, and more. The advantage of doing that is it makes creating content toolboxes and local citations for each location much simpler.

This is something my company, BirdEye, helps dentists create because it gives each office a better chance to have its location listed on the first page of search results when people search for dentists near each specific location. Talk to your team or web company about doing the same for your practice if you have multiple locations. Also, feel free to connect with me if you have any questions or need direction.

Make sure your practice is listed on the most important listing websites for dentists.

If you do a Google search for your practice right now, at least two or three of the results on the first page will be local citation websites. Thus, in addition to helping you appear on the first page of general search results, having robust, accurate local citations—particularly listing websites that are most important to dental practices and which are more likely to appear on the first page of search results—also helps you control more of the first page of search results when people search specifically for you.

Many of the most important sites are the same for all dentists because they influence search rankings more than others and often appear on the first page of results when people search specifically for you. Other sites are important to some practices but not others depending on the type or location or your practice. Additionally, this list is dynamic. New sites will appear and others will disappear. To find an updated and comprehensive list of the most important sites for your practice, visit the resources page at DrLenTau.com.

"A good reputation for yourself and your company is an invaluable asset not reflected in the balance sheets."

—Li Ka-Shing

Some sites will increase in importance while others will decrease in importance. Because this area of reputation marketing is so important while at the same time being tedious, time-consuming, dynamic, and specialized, I highly recommend every dentist use reputation marketing software to keep your local citations consistent from one dashboard. This way, you don't have to manually update dozens of websites when anything changes. You can just log into one dashboard, make a change, upload an image or video, or add information, and it'll get automatically delivered to all the important websites at once. And you can get back to serving your patients well and running your business.

No matter how you manage your local citations, it's important to understand not only what you're doing but why you're doing it. This way when things change or new websites come to market, you'll know whether the changes or new websites are relevant to your practice and what to do if they are. That's why I will not just give you a list of websites and let you go. Instead, I'll show you how to identify the most important listing websites for *your* specific practice so you can ensure whoever is managing your local citations is serving you well. After you go through this part, you can visit the resources page at DrLenTau.com/ BookResources to get a comprehensive and updated list of local citations and optimize the ones that are most relevant to you.

You can also sign up for my free email newsletter at DrLenTau.com to get the best and latest news about reputation marketing sent right to your inbox.

The Most Important Listing Websites for *All* Dental Practices

The most important listing websites are Google, Yelp!, Facebook, Healthgrades, Bing Places, SuperPages.com, YouTube.com, Zocdoc, RateMDs, Vitals, and YellowPages.com. Having an accurate presence on these websites is critical, especially with Google because it is by far the most popular site people use to find dentists.

Google will highlight your Google listing, which is now called Google My Business (GMB). Claiming and optimizing your GMB page should be a high priority for all practices. In addition to Google, at least two and likely more of the other sites I referenced above will appear on the first page of Google search results when someone searches for you.

GOOGLE MY BUSINESS

If you look at your Google My Business page and it asks, "Are you the owner?" it means your page is unclaimed. You need to claim the listing to reap the most benefits from it. When you are in your dental office, click on the link that says, "Own this business?" and follow the steps to claim your business. Google will want to call your office to give you a code to confirm you are the business owner. They can also send you a postcard, but that obviously takes longer.

Once you have claimed your GMB profile and established an address and phone number (one that is local and permanent) take the following steps to help your profile appear in the local 3-pack.

1. **Enter accurate data into your profile**—This includes business name, hours of operation, phone number, website, appointment URL, etc.

2. **Verify your dental business**—Note: it takes approximately five to seven business days to receive your Google verification code to claim your Google My Business listing.

3. **Make sure you are adding the correct primary and secondary categories**—Be very specific with your primary category so Google can quickly determine what your business is about. Secondary categories can be treatment-specific, such as "emergency dental services." The primary category would be "dentist" or "dental clinic."

4. **Add at least five relevant photos**—To take it to the next level, geo-optimize your images and add videos, too (see more on photos and videos below).

5. **Consistently manage and respond to reviews**—Reviews are one of Google's top local ranking factors, especially those on your GMB profile. To increase reviews, you can use review software like BirdEye.

6. **Share content from your website on your GMB post option**—This is great for local brand awareness.

Your ultimate goal should be to enhance your Google My Business profile by completing as much information as possible.

In time, your hard work will reap the reward of a steady stream of new patients selecting your practice.

PHOTOS AND VIDEOS

Remember that a picture is worth a thousand words. Along with acquiring a steady stream of 5star reviews, publishing high-quality content, monitoring your citations, protecting your reputation, and connecting with other local businesses, updating the photos and videos on your Google My Business listing should be a priority for you or anybody who optimizes your online presence.

But don't take my word for it, take theirs:

- "60% of consumers say local search results with good images capture their attention and push them toward a decision." —BrightLocal
- "90% of customers are more likely to visit a business with photos on Google." —GoogleMyBiz
- "If video and text are both available on the same page, 72% of people will watch the video to learn about a product or service rather than read the text."—HubSpot

Moral of the story: Go update your photos and add some video to your GMB listing. It's a minimal-effort, low-risk, high-reward way to separate your practice from the competition.

GOOGLE POSTS

Google launched this posting feature in 2016 to help make local business listings a lot stronger and powerful. When Google Posts first launched during the presidential election, it didn't gain much traction; in fact, most of us thought Google would do away with it by the end of the year. Now, more than three years later[10], the feature is one of the most important pieces of your SEO and overall content strategy.

Google Posts are short, 100- to 300-word posts accompanied by a photo or video. The intention of these free posts is to highlight sales, promotions, or events for your dental office. These posts (with an exception of events) expire after 7 days, forcing businesses to continuously post fresh content. A user can view posts from the overview of your GMB listing. You can scroll left to right up to ten posts, or you can go to the "posts" tab of the GMB listing to view all posts. Complete with Call To Action (CTA) options and insights for each post, Google Posts, which helps generate more organic clicks, give businesses an entirely new way to share content with their local customers.

Google Posts are a great way to improve your overall SEO strategy:

- Organic clicks on CTA buttons will build up your page rankings.
- You can increase traffic to other forms of content on your site. What's more, users who are already searching for your business or businesses like you are likely to be further down the conversion funnel, and thus more valuable, compared to those who you are hoping to capture through traditional ad campaigns.

---

10 Although Google Posts were originally displayed more prominently in the Business Profile, they have dropped to a lower position, decreasing their overall effectiveness. Regardless, their placement on mobile is still very prominent, and the click-through rates are still impressive. What's more, users who are already searching for your business or businesses like yours are likely to be further down the conversion funnel, and thus more valuable, compared to those you are hoping to capture through traditional ad campaigns. The ability to reach your ideal audience when and where it matters most can be extremely beneficial, especially when you can showcase your expertise.

- You can link a Google Post to a form to collect user information and increase traffic long term to areas of your site such as your blog.

Google Posts deliver location-specific, timely, and actionable content to boost the right engagement with the right audience. Posting consistently will help build location authority (the power to rank in local searches) for your listing. Google tracks engagement, so having organic clicks on CTA buttons can build up your page ranking as well as signal to Google that your content is highly relevant to users. At least indirectly, an increase in Location Authority should lead to better ranking.

For Google Posts, remember to:

- Have a strong CTA at the end of each post.
- Properly track visits to your website.
- Use high-quality photos; if you don't have any, use stock.
- Create custom landing pages to match the post content.

Now that you understand the importance of incorporating Google Posts into your marketing strategy, do you have the right action plan set in place to manage them efficiently? If not, reach out to me and I can help connect you with companies that help you with this new way to promote your business on Google.

While Google is by far the most popular search engine people use to find dentists, millions of people also search Bing every day. While it's not even close to the volume as Google (The joke that "Bing" stands for But It's Not Google …), your Bing Local listing will help you when people search there. The other sites are all popular listing sites with significant influence in search results across the board.

I include Yelp! with a bit of hesitation. It will almost always be on the first page of search results for your practice. Yelp! also has the reviews associated with Apple iOS devices, so if you search on Apple Maps on your iOS device or ask Siri for a recommendation, the search results will be heavily based on Yelp! results. Yelp! also powers reviews for Bing and has its reviews show on MapQuest and other important sites.

Because of that, having your NAP information accurate in Yelp! is important. That said, Yelp! tends to have a challenging relationship with dental practices, to put it lightly, because Yelp! filters reviews using a secret algorithm that appears to many people to result in inconsistent results and filter out many honest, legitimate reviews by patients. Yelp! contends that it filters reviews based on a user's history with Yelp!, although many dentists suggest this does not always appear to be the case. Yelp! also contends its filtering practice is designed to protect consumers. In addition, Yelp! highlights your competitors' listings prominently on your page, especially competitors with premium listings. Thus, patients who search for you are directed to your competitors.

For these reasons, I suggest dentists focus on Google reviews and only send trusted, experienced Yelp! users to Yelp! for reviews. You can identify these by posting a sign in your office asking experienced Yelp! users to talk with you about providing feedback and asking those who do to give you a review with a goal of collecting 20 to 30 great Yelp! reviews that are not filtered out. This is the point at which Yelp! will start to work better for you. If you ask Yelpers to write a Google review, where do you think they will write it? Yelp! of course.

In the meantime, your Google reviews will be much easier to get and more impactful for your practice. Beyond that, I suggest you just make sure your Yelp! listing has accurate NAP information, and otherwise concentrate your time and effort in other places. Dentists often ask me if they should leave their listing unclaimed or even delete their Yelp! listing and the answer is absolutely not since it is an extremely trusted citation.

Finally, in addition to these sites, you should also include any listing websites that come up on the first few pages of search results when you search for your practice on your list of highest-priority local citations to optimize. If you didn't do it when I suggested doing so in the Preface, try it for yourself now. Open a private web browser, called an "Incognito" window in Google's Chrome browser or a private window in Apple's Safari browser.

This is important because web browsers get to know you based on your past searches, so they might return different information to you than they would to a patient who has never looked at your webpage, social media accounts, or listings. Run a Google search for your name. On the first page of results, you will see your Google My Business listing and likely two or three of the other sites. Smaller practices may see four or five listing websites on the first page of Google search results for their name. If you have a practice name that is different than your name, repeat this process for your practice name.

Additional Important Local Citations

Claiming and optimizing your listing on only the top citation sites is a good start, but it is far from enough. Specifically, although claiming and optimizing the top local citations help if people search specifically for you and see them appear with accurate information, if you want to be noticed by Google and other search engines when people are searching for a dentist in your area, you need to be listed accurately on a critical mass of sites indexed by search engines.

Through our research and experience at BirdEye, we have found it most impactful for your search results if your practice has consistent local citations on more than 50 websites; I provided a brief overview of some of them earlier. If you choose to do this manually, these are additional sites we recommend claiming and optimizing. You can find links to where you can claim and update these listings and more on the resources page at DrLenTau.com.

Some are more important than others for practices, but they are all indexed by search engines and part of a good overall search engine optimization strategy. For example, Zocdoc is a useful listing for local citation purposes, but can be hit or miss for direct benefits beyond that, such as for attracting patients directly from the site. Insurance-based practices in big cities tend to get more value from that perspective, but most other practices will not get much benefit. If your patient mix comes mostly from Zocdoc, you will end up with an insurance-heavy mix. It does not do much for me because I do not accept insurance.

To find the most important local citations for you, search for your practice and see which ones come up on the first few pages. Those will be the most important for you. It is really that simple. Add those sites to the list of local citations you need to claim and optimize. Of course, this is much easier to do if you use software such as BirdEye (or one of several I listed in the Introduction) because you can enter the information you want to appear in one dashboard and be confident that it will be consistent across all relevant sites.

If you prefer to claim and optimize your local citations on your own, the rest of this chapter will show you exactly what you need to do. Although I highly recommend outsourcing this task because it is time-consuming and each local citation has a slightly different process, it is still important that you know the process so you can be a more informed consumer and ensure whoever is helping you does so in a way that will help you actually get found online.

For those who would like to consider using a service to help with their consistency online, there are a number of companies that offer directory cleanup. These companies include Yext, Moz Local, Whitespark, BrightLocal, and Sweet IQ. The cost of these services can range from anywhere from $20 to $100 dollars per month.

Claim, review, and update your information on all relevant listing websites.

Once you have your list of local citations, the next step is to claim, review, and update your information, especially your NAP information, on each site and make sure it is consistent and optimized for search engines.

Although some of the listing sites can be challenging to navigate, there's usually a free registration process for each site where you can sign up, "claim" the listing as your practice, confirm your identity as the owner, and update the information. Confirming your identity is often done by the site sending you a verification code by automated phone call to a known number, email to a known email address, or snail mail to a known postal mailing address.

Companies can do all of this for you, of course. If you choose BirdEye, you will get citation claiming as part of its services.

INDUSTRY INSIGHTS

I saw Dr. Leonard Tau speak in 2016. What I learned from his presentation became the basis of how my practice asked for patient feedback from then on.

As we all know now, online reviews are the biggest criteria for patients when choosing a dental practice. But back in 2016, asking patients for a review was as awkward as going on a blind date. Dr. Leonard Tau taught me we should not ask for reviews. Instead, we should ask for "feedback." I immediately put that into practice at my practice, Dental Smiles Dentistry in Denton, Texas. We had been using review capture software but weren't getting much progress before I saw Len speak.

Since then, our reviews and SEO both skyrocketed. We're at the top of the Google map pack, and our website is right at the top of the first page of search results when people search for "dentist Denton, TX," "best dentist in Denton, TX" and similar search terms. It's incredible.

Len also taught us the best ways to ask for feedback so our patients feel comfortable doing so and putting their thoughts in their own words. Our patients love to give us their own feedback because it makes them feel heard and helpful.

Before putting Len's processes in place, we were not getting the highest return on our investment in review software. Since we implemented his strategies, the effectiveness of our review capture software has increased significantly. That was another lesson I learned from Len: The review software you use is only as effective as the strategy you employ to get patient "feedback."

—**Glenn Vo**, *Denton Smiles Dentistry and NiftyThriftyDentists.com*

Additional Words of Caution

Some local citation websites ask you to pay for listings, either to have a "premium" listing or as the only option. In most cases, I suggest opting *against* paying for citations or even a premium listing on a site that offers a free option for two important reasons.

First, paying for listings puts you in a position to have to keep paying the listing website or risk losing search engine influence from that site. Becoming reliant on any paid advertising relationships, including paying for a premium listing, puts those listing websites in control of your marketing. They can raise their prices whenever they want. If you rely on that advertising to get patients, you're almost forced to just keep paying, at least until you find a better way (like this plan). Building search engine influence by optimizing free listing options is a much more stable option and has proven to be effective for me and thousands of dentists with whom I have worked over a decade.

Second, you could achieve much greater impact by directing the money you would spend on a paid listing toward outsourcing listing management to a company like I listed above or BirdEye to ensure you have accurate and consistent local citations on more than 60 directories without you or a team member having to manually manage and monitor the citations, a challenging and time-consuming endeavor.

Additionally, never pay a third party claiming to be able to manipulate search results to get a specific citation or other piece of news about you off the first page of search results. This happens often with Yelp! because of how frustrating that site has been for many dentists. This is a complete scam, and you most certainly will end up losing a lot of money.

"Do not leave your reputation to chance or gossip; it is your life's artwork and you must craft it, hone it, and display it with the care of an artist."

—**Robert Greene**, *The 48 Laws of Power*

Because Yelp! will almost always appear on the first page of results when people search for you, and its algorithm filters out a high percentage of reviews, dentists sometimes get swindled into paying a company to get their Yelp! listing off the first page. It happens all the time. Dentists get 10 Yelp! reviews. Eight of them are great. Two are bad. Seven of the eight great reviews are filtered out because they are from inexperienced Yelp! users.

It is frustrating because dentists know all eight reviews are legitimate. They will get a phone call from a company that says: "I notice you have a couple of bad Yelp! reviews and the good reviews are all filtered out. When people search for your practice, Yelp! is on the first page of results, but we can get it off the front page by pushing other content up. You cannot control Yelp! but we can help you control where Yelp! appears."

This simply does not work. If Yelp! is on the first page of your search results, which it is for almost every dental practice, it will stay there no matter what you do, so your best response is to focus on building Google reviews and asking only trusted Yelp! users to review you on Yelp! with a goal of getting twenty or thirty unfiltered Yelp! reviews. There's no way to get it off the first page. It will never happen. Trying to get it moved is a waste of money.

Outsource wisely. Some companies tell you they can manage your local citations and that they can get you on dozens of websites. But the websites they use are not indexed by search engines, so they are not helpful. If you are going to outsource, which you know I highly recommend, make sure the company you outsource to understands your practice and its unique place in the market and takes care of the most relevant local citations that will be indexed by search engines. If the local citations they help you with (in a one-size-fits-all approach) are not the most relevant to help you get found online in your unique situation, you will not achieve as high a return compared to one that optimizes the process for your specific practice.

Next we'll talk about how to set up a simple but effective website to help you get found online. Before doing so, take a few minutes to go through these exercises to identify the most important local citations for your practice and put a plan together to claim and optimize them to help you move up the results when a patient is searching for a dentist in your area.

Top Dental Citations

Take a look at the top dental citations for dentists according to BrightLocal. Some of these sites are paid, and some are free.

- Zocdoc.com

- Vitals.com
- Wellness.com
- 1800dentist.com
- UCompareHealth.com
- TheDentistHub.com
- HealthPofs.com
- Doctor.com
- DoctorOogle.com
- EveryDentist.com

The Importance of Local Citations

A 2018 study conducted by BrightLocal looked at citations and their impact on local pack rankings. From 122,125 local directories across 26 different industries, BrightLocal looked at the correlation between a business's number and variety of citations and its ranking.

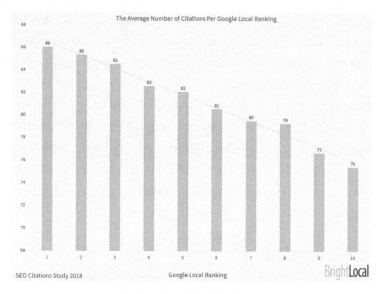

Image Credit: BrightLocal

Here are some of the key findings uncovered by the study:
- Local businesses who rank in the top 10 positions in Google Local have an average of 81 citations.
- 5% of local businesses don't have any of the most popular citation sites.
- Businesses ranked No. 1 in the Google Local Finder have an average of 86 citations. Businesses ranked No. 10 have an average of 75.

BrightLocal also conducted a survey of industry experts in 2018 and asked about their thoughts on the importance of local citations and local ranking.
- 90% of experts believe accurate citations are important to local search ranking.
- 9% of experts say that that industry relevance is "very important" when choosing citation sites, and 86% say that same about local relevance.

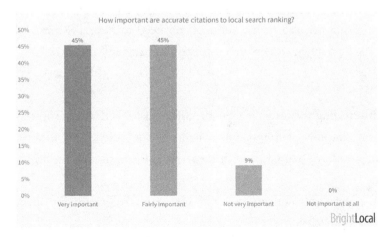

Image Credit: BrightLocal

Here is what some well-respected local SEO experts have to say on the importance of citations.

> "Today, citations are seen as a fundamental element of local SEO. If you don't have them, you can't compete locally, and awareness of this is high. Because of this, a greater percentage of businesses are getting this right first time, and so these signals don't make as much competitive difference as they used to."
>
> —Myles Anderson

> "Much as citations became table stakes over the last couple of years, reviews now appear to be on their way to becoming table stakes as well."
>
> —David Mihm

> "There always has been, and always will be, benefit in getting your listings 'good enough' on the basic sites and sites geared to your niche. Especially when those sites are also review sites, as you need to have a listing on a given site before customers can review you there."
>
> —Phil Rozek

Interestingly enough, when BrightLocal looked at consumer trust in local citations, it found that consumers *do* look at the information online and have had issues with incorrect information about businesses online.

- 93% of consumers say they are frustrated by incorrect information in online directories.

- 80% of consumers lose trust in local businesses if they see incorrect or inconsistent contact details or business names online.
- In the last 12 months, 71% of consumers had a negative experience because of incorrect local business information found online.
- In the last year, 22% of consumers visited the wrong location for a business because the address was incorrect online.

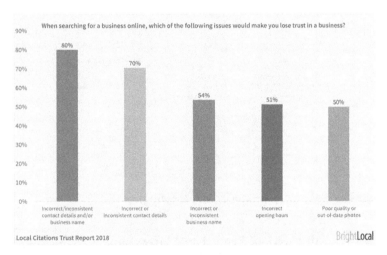

Image Credit: BrightLocal

Look what would happen if someone were to find incorrect information on these online directories. They could potentially not want to use your business, as 78% of men and 62% of women say that they would look elsewhere. It sure makes you think about what information is online about your dental practice.

The most important takeaway is that you can't just set it and forget it—you need to keep on top of your online presence and make changes when your information changes, especially when your office moves to a new location.

Image Credit: BrightLocal

To recap this section, here's a real-life example of something that happened to a practice I was recently advising through BirdEye. The business manager thought its practice was ranked No. 1, since she was searching in a regular browser from the office location. But when I searched for "dentist Mt Holly North Carolina," she was quite surprised to see that her office was not ranked in the top three despite the fact that it had 124 Google reviews. The office was also using Lighthouse 360 and had 1170 Rate A Biz reviews more on this later). Some of the dentists who were ranked above them had far fewer Google reviews. When I ran my citation scanner, here is what I found:

The office's listings are filled with a lot of inconsistencies related to the name of the practice. A couple of sites have the associate doctor listed, but the office moved three years ago and the citations have never been updated, so the address is wrong on many of the sites. This can lead to confusion not only with people searching online but also with Google, which ultimately prevents the practice from ranking higher. If your practice looks like this, it's time for some fixes.

Local Citation Exercises

1. In a private browser, run a Google search for "dentist in" and "best dentist in" followed by your city, town, or neighborhood. Do you appear on the first page? If not, who does? What do they do differently than you?

2. In a private browser, run a Google search for your name and practice name. What information comes up? What listing websites are on the first three pages?

3. Make a list of your most important local citation websites.

4. Go to the resources page at DrLenTau.com/BookResources to access links to the most important listing websites.
5. If you have any questions, connect with me. I would be happy to help you analyze what local citations are most important for you.

CHAPTER 3

Using Online Reviews to Get Found

Online reviews serve two important purposes. First, they help you rise up Google's search results, especially when you are getting regular positive Google reviews. Second, they help you get found in a way that encourages people to become your patients. I call them "trustamonials" as they cause people to trust your business based on what others are saying about you.

In this chapter, I will discuss how they can impact your position on search results. In the next section, when we discuss getting found in a compelling way, I will give you a simple plan to regularly collect reviews that show people why you should be their dentist. The plan will work to help you accomplish both getting found and doing so in a compelling way.

INDUSTRY INSIGHTS

After working in dentistry for two decades, I was told, "Please get reviews from your patients." When I asked, no one really had a clear answer on how to accomplish such a task. So, I talked to website companies, other businesses, colleagues, and such. Most people just said, "Get a Google or Yelp! review."

In 2001, we had our first team meeting scheduled to discuss getting our first reviews. The employees knew that our potential patients are shopping online and that those people would relate to our patient testimonials. Website companies expressed that we need to be on the first page or better yet, the top three dentists on the list. At the end of the meeting, we were all pumped to have a bunch of happy patients potentially posting about us online.

Unfortunately, after much effort, we didn't receive any! We discovered patients didn't know how, and frankly, we didn't either. We tried everything we knew—we verbally asked patients, we sent emails requesting their opinion, and we texted links telling people how much we would appreciate their thoughts. We went to Google Maps and showed patients how to post a review and so forth. It seemed like for the amount of effort we put into it that we should have had better results.

Through all the efforts that we tried, there was little that gave us better results. We knew that 99% of patients had great things to say about us, from "Best cleaning ever" and "You guys make coming to the dental office fun!" to "You guys are always so gentle and thorough."

While these compliments are *great* to hear, we needed them online. If you don't believe in the power of reviews (good and bad), go do some online shopping and tell me which product you buy. Notice how more powerful it is to see 100 reviews for a product versus one with only 22 reviews. In addition, did you skip the "Sponsored" ad? I do, because I know that the company paid to be placed on the top of the list. I usually scroll down to the top three products underneath the sponsored ones. Getting consistent online reviews is truly the greatest marketing strategy you could do to grow your dental practice.

—Heidi Mount, Hawaii

Google Reviews: The Most Important for Getting Found

Simply put, Google reviews are the most important reviews on the internet because Google is the most important site on the internet. Its reviews influence where you appear in search results.

If you have consistent local citations, a lot of Google reviews, and are regularly adding more great Google reviews, you are much more likely to be included in the map results when someone searches for a dentist in their area.

When someone searches for you, Google will include your Google My Business profile on the first page of the search results, including your Google reviews.

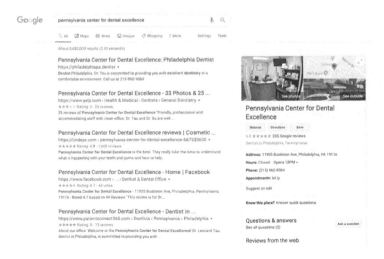

Google knows how important reviews are to consumers, and values Google reviews highly because it wants to provide the most useful results to its users and earn more searches, which leads to Google earning more advertising revenue. Because of this, I encourage dentists to focus all their review-collecting efforts on getting Google reviews on a regular basis. Be sure to take advantage of your Google My Business listing. On a regular basis, I interact with dentists who fail to capitalize on this free advertising.

Google reviews are much more important than Yelp! reviews.

When I train dentists at conferences, people are often surprised to learn that Google reviews are much more powerful and important than Yelp! reviews. Although Yelp! has been the most known site for online reviews, it is also the most frustrating for many businesses. Fortunately, Yelp! is not very important for most dental practices because it is not a site most patients use to find a dentist, at least for practices in most cities.

Most patients ask family and friends for a referral, check their insurance plan's provider list, or search Google for a new dentist. When they search Google, your Google reviews will appear right next to your contact information. Your Yelp! listing might appear lower on the search results, but at that point, they already know you and have seen your Google reviews.

If you end up with dozens of great reviews on Google, with new ones being added on a regular basis, people will see your Google reviews in their search results and be less influenced by Yelp! reviews. Additionally, although Yelp! has a significant track record, and usually on the first Google's search results for every practice it has been losing some of its clout recently as more and more consumers are becoming aware of accusation of review manipulation. It's even less important for practices in smaller cities where there are not as many people using Yelp!

Yelp! also has been known to filter reviews, and there's no way to know whether your efforts to get people to leave you reviews on Yelp! will make a difference. The site says this is to avoid manipulating the system; however, their settings filter out many legitimate reviews.

It has long been believed that Yelp! provides favorable treatment to companies who advertise with them and filters more reviews, especially positive ones, for companies who do not. To be clear, the company has denied this, and it has never been proven; however, this speaks to the level of frustration people have with felt, in particular with the way Yelp! filters reviews.

I have studied Yelp! extensively and give classes called Help on Yelp! and do not believe that they favor companies that pay for advertising. It has specific rules and algorithms that you must follow and understand. If you do not, you most certainly will be frustrated. If you go in understanding how things work, you will probably be able to take advantage of Yelp!

Many dentists complain that Yelp! filters more positive reviews than negative ones. For example, I do not do any business with Yelp! other than to claim and optimize my listing. Over the years, however, I have collected 67 Yelp! reviews as of this writing. Yelp! filtered out 38 of them, removed four, and displays only 25 of them. This equates to a 3-star rating, which honestly sucks, but I have resigned myself to the fact that I am unable to get Yelp! reviews to stay out of the filter as my patients are not active Yelpers.

With my practice, eight of the 38 filtered reviews are 1-star reviews. The rest are 5-star reviews. But those reviewers don't have a lot of experience with or connections on Yelp!, so the algorithm hides them, resulting in my rating being inaccurate. Even worse, if someone decides to display the filtered reviews, Yelp! displays all the negative reviews first and forces people to click through three additional pages to see all the positive reviews it filters.

Yelp! is not very big in Philadelphia, so it does not make much of an impact on my practice, but the site is a big frustration for many dentists. Every month I get a report from Yelp! letting me know how many visitors have seen my Yelp! page, and last month it was 30 people. I also get a report from Google about my Google My Business listing and it is about 1,000 visitors per month. A big difference.

If Yelp! is big in your area (California, Chicago, Miami, Dallas, NYC, Seattle, and some other select cities), it could help to earn a number of positive Yelp! reviews. But it can be a frustrating process at best. Your time is better spent collecting reviews on other sites. I would much rather you focus on Google than Yelp! reviews. I know many dentists who absolutely swear by Yelp! and get tons of patients every month from the site. One dentist in particular is Joshua Austin in San Antonio. We both talk about reputation marketing and inform the uninformed about Yelp! and its bad reputation online. Stay tuned to for making Yelp! more successful for your practice.

With Google reviews, unless you are running afoul of Google's rules, such as by asking people to leave you reviews while they are in your office, virtually all of your reviews will be shown to people on the first page of search results for your name or practice name.

I suggest practices try to increase their Yelp! reviews *without* setting up a check-in offer. You can offer an incentive for check-in such as a Starbucks gift card or credit on account or even a whitening pen. When you do this and a patient checks in, Yelp! will send them a review request on their own later in the day. If completed, this review has a greater chance of sticking in the recommended section.

Google Review Rules and Guidelines

Although Google reviews have been much more beneficial to dentists than Yelp!, Google does have its own review policies that all businesses and all software platforms need to comply with.

In late 2017, many businesses ran afoul of their rules, some inadvertently, and saw Google remove many of their reviews. As with anything done according to an automated algorithm, Google's removal was not perfect, so many legitimate reviews got deleted, too.

As with Yelp!, it is frustrating when you work hard to deliver a great experience to your patients and earn a positive review only to have it deleted. Frustration grew in late 2017, because many people associated Google's mass deletion with Yelp!'s filtering and removal.

Fortunately, that is not the case. Like Yelp!, Google's review removal is done by a machine following a set of rules. It is not done manually. Everything is automated. If the machine comes across a review that triggers suspicion according to the criteria, it automatically deletes that review. The machine does not discriminate; it examines a piece of data and makes a decision.

Unlike Yelp!, Google's policies and actions are concrete enough to give us a useful understanding of how to lower the chances your legitimate reviews will be deleted. This is important for businesses like dental offices, which rely on the power of reviews to attract patients.

To help clients better understand how to protect their Google reviews, my colleagues and I at BirdEye tested a subset of Google data in late 2017. We started with Google's published review policy and posted review violation criteria on Google's community forums in order to demystify Google reviews as best as possible.

We then tested the most common scenarios against our own sample data and, based on these results, came up with best practices for businesses to follow that will help protect their hard-earned reviews from deletion.

We summarized our findings in an article to help correct much of the misinformation on the internet about why Google removes reviews.

You can find a link to the article on the resources page at DrLenTau.com/BookResources. Below is a summary of the relevant common violation criteria for dentists, along with the data and suggested best practices.

COMMON GOOGLE REVIEW VIOLATIONS

GOOGLE REVIEWS VIOLATION NO. 1:

Your listing has received a lot of reviews within a short amount of time.

BirdEye Data Analysis: Our data clearly shows a high correlation to rapid increases in new reviews being tied to review removal. In other words, if a practice sees a rapid increase in the number of reviews received in a relatively short amount of time, this will likely be flagged by Google's algorithm and potentially cause reviews to be deleted.

Best Practices: If you are asking for reviews manually, get organized so you either ask every patient using the strategies I teach you in the next part, or to ask a certain number of patients each day. This way your reviews come on a consistent basis, rather than rapidly increasing and decreasing when you ask inconsistently.

If you are using software such as BirdEye to help you, ask whether it allows you to limit the number of review requests you send during a period of time by setting up something called a drip campaign. This feature "drips" out your review requests over time instead of sending them in bulk to help you limit your risk of being flagged by Google. Using such an automated program with a drip campaign to ask all patients to share feedback on Google is the best bet for maintaining consistent review volume over time without having to worry about inadvertently running afoul of Google's guidelines.

GOOGLE REVIEWS VIOLATION NO. 2:

The person reviewing you has a completely blank profile and has no activity on that profile before or after they left a review.

BirdEye Data Analysis: Our data shows that a substantial proportion of reviews from inactive or non-existing Google accounts are deleted. These show up to Google as "Google User" reviews, a label used by Google when the Google+ account of the reviewer no longer exists.

Best Practices: This is a red flag for Google because of bad practices it has seen from some SEO companies. These companies create Google accounts, use them to post reviews, and then delete the accounts. Google has also modified policies and now requires a Google account to leave a review. A reviewer may want to post the review as anonymous, and the only option to do that is to delete their Google Plus account.

Unfortunately, you have limited control over this; our recommendation is to always provide a great service so patients feel confident leaving you a review using their name and not as an anonymous review. In 2018, Google eliminated all old reviews left before the establishment of Google+. As an early adopter of reviews going back to 2009 and 2010, I lost about 35 reviews that were left by "A Google User" since back then there was no way to attach a name to a review.

GOOGLE REVIEWS VIOLATION NO. 3:

You hired an agency to solicit reviews for you, and they are using methods against the guidelines.

BirdEye Data Analysis: When someone hires a company to solicit reviews for them, this becomes obvious because reviews come in bunches, often from similar addresses or far from your practice address.

Best Practices: Never hire a company to create reviews for you. BirdEye will never create reviews for a customer, nor will we ever create fake accounts to use for review posting. If a company offers this to you, please do not engage with them. The only software we recommend is similar to what BirdEye does, which is *automating the process of getting authentic reviews from your real patients.* Other companies such as Podium and Swell CX offer software similar to BirdEye. Just make sure you are using a legitimate company. A long time ago, I used a company that called my patients on the phone after their appointments to gather feedback about their experiences and then wrote the review online as if they were the patient. But they did this for dental offices all over the country, so the same reviewer had reviews in Philadelphia, Seattle, Dallas, etc. Guess what? Google caught wind and deleted all of the reviews left by this company.

GOOGLE REVIEWS VIOLATION NO. 4:

The person who wrote the review is a manager of your page or works for you.

BirdEye Data Analysis: It is usually obvious not only to Google when your reviews were written by a biased person. (Patients can tell, too.) Even one review from someone associated with your practice diminishes the credibility of all your authentic reviews—before, of course, it is removed completely. The bottom line is getting your employees to review your business has no benefit.

Best Practices: Please ensure your employees do not leave reviews for your practice or post reviews that can be considered advertising your services. These will surely be flagged and removed and could actually hurt your reputation with potential patients before they get removed. In fact, if you wrote a review for yourself, which I come across quite often, go ahead and remove it as well.

GOOGLE REVIEWS VIOLATION NO. 5:

Your reviews appear to be spam. Here are some reasons your authentic reviews could appear spam-like to Google:

- The person wrote the review from the same device or IP address you sign into to manage your local listing.
- The person wrote the review from the same device or IP address as other users who left you reviews.
- You offer incentives for people to write reviews.

BirdEye Data Analysis: Our data shows that in more than 90% of instances, the reviews coming from the same device or IP address get deleted by Google. These IP address issues could be due to several reasons:

- Your business uses a mobile kiosk (on-site review station via business iPad, computer, etc.) to collect reviews.
- You have free Wi-Fi and are asking for reviews before the consumer leaves the premises.
- You offer incentives. This could mean offering discounts or coupons in exchange for reviews, paying an agency or person to write reviews for you, or having employees write reviews for your business.

Best Practices: If you are soliciting reviews manually, let the patient know you will be sending them a review request later that day when they are home. This way, you do not risk multiple patients entering a review while in your waiting room, building lobby, or parking lot.

If you treat multiple family members and want two adults to leave you a review, be careful to not have both review you from their home. This may trigger Google's spam filter because both reviews will come from the same location. Thus, either ask only one person to leave you a review or, if you have an especially good relationship with them, ask one to leave you one from their work.

Using software such as BirdEye helps because it automates the process of sending review requests via SMS and email, so your customers can post using their own devices. BirdEye also lets you delay delivery of the review request to protect you from having multiple people reviewing from your waiting room, building lobby, or parking lot.

When I analyzed the reviews I lost last year, I discovered that one of them was the demo review from an actual patient who I filmed in my office. Google knows where the reviews are being left. So be careful—don't try to circumvent the rules because you can lose reviews, which can hurt your business and ruin all the hard work you and your team have done.

GOOGLE REVIEWS VIOLATION NO. 6:

The person tried to post a review for you several times on different dates.

For example, a customer wrote a review on August 5, and it got filtered, so they tried again on October 10.

BirdEye Data Analysis: This could happen if you ask a patient to review you instantly after a service or transaction, and then a few weeks later, you ask them again.

Best Practices: Managing your online reputation requires an understanding of best practices on how often you should solicit reviews from your consumers. If you are doing this manually, input a note for when a review was requested in their file so you do not inadvertently ask customers multiple times.

If you are using software to help you, make sure it has a feature to control this. BirdEye customers can set limits on how often review requests are sent to each customer. As a best practice, we recommend review requests are limited to one time in 30 days and only after the service has been provided.

GOOGLE REVIEWS VIOLATION NO. 7:

The person reviewing you has also reviewed multiple other practices with the same name.

BirdEye Data Analysis: This can happen if your business has several locations and a patient reviews all of them. If the reviews are not specific and unique to the location, they may be filtered. This can also happen if you have two pages for the same location.

Best Practices: Ask only actual patients for reviews. If you have multiple locations, only send a review request from the location they visited. If you are doing this manually from a central location, make sure they have request links for each location clearly labeled, so they do not inadvertently send the wrong link.

If you are using software such as BirdEye to help you, make sure it has the ability to provide a custom check-in URL and location-specific review request flow to ensure customers review the correct location.

GOOGLE REVIEWS VIOLATION NO. 8:

The reviews link that you are providing customers pre-populates the review form in any way.

BirdEye Data Analysis: This could mean pre-populating star ratings or review text for customers, which can lead to a review bias such as a falsely inflated star rating.

Best Practices: Avoid sending any links or using any software that pre-populates the review in any way. BirdEye does not pre-populate review requests with ratings or content and does not offer this option.

Rather, BirdEye makes it easy for your customers to reach your business' profile on Google and write their own authentic feedback. It facilitates and supports the review process but does not influence the review. Be sure you do not use any software that does.

GOOGLE REVIEWS VIOLATION NO. 9:

Your address has changed. You cannot take it for granted that Google will transfer reviews when a business address changes.

BirdEye Data Analysis: This can happen if your business moves and you do not update your address online. Your online presence is priceless and should be managed with great care. It is critical that your business information, particularly your Name, Address and Phone number (NAP) in Google and across the internet is always up to date and accurate, or you risk moving down in search results and losing great customer reviews.

Best Practices: When you move or change your phone number, it is important to update it on every listing website possible, especially the most important ones. If you do this manually, this makes it especially important that you have a folder on your computer or server dedicated to citations where you will keep relevant images, documents, and spreadsheets.

Include a spreadsheet with links to your most relevant local citations, and update them all as soon as your address changes. If you use software like BirdEye to help, be sure to update your address in your dashboard because BirdEye will keep your local citations consistent on more than fifty sites automatically. This way, you can just login to your BirdEye dashboard, change your address once, and BirdEye will handle the rest.

More Considerations and Best Practices

With so much on our plates running a practice and treating patients, it is easy to inadvertently violate Google's rules, or those of another review site. These are the most common review-removal issues we have observed. Here are some additional issues I have observed helping our BirdEye clients and how BirdEye has responded to several recent Google changes. These are good guidelines to follow no matter how you manage your local citations and online reviews.

Are you sending review requests only to a subset of patients, such as promoters?

We do not have any data to suggest that Google penalizes practices that send review invitations to only promoters, nor do we believe it is possible for Google to track that. That said, we have checked with Google's product team, and they did confirm that they discourage practices from using sentiment pre-checks to ensure only positive reviews are requested.

BirdEye's default platform configuration is to disable sentiment precheck. In 2018, we started educating all our businesses to move away from sending review requests to promoters only. Google no longer allows software companies to "gate" reviews. Review gating is the process of filtering candidates before asking them to leave you a review. Normally companies do this by sending all customers an email or text and first asking them if they had a positive or negative experience.

If customers had a positive experience, companies ask them to leave a review on Google but if they had a negative experience, they are prompted to leave private feedback and are never sent the option to leave a review publicly. If you are using a service that still uses a "gate," you are seriously risking losing reviews. I know a practice that had more than 30 Google reviews and was using a third-party software that was still review gating. Google was alerted and that business lost all, I repeat *all* of its reviews. It also basically flagged the account for potential future issues potentially.

Do you have reviews in other places online?

If you have tons of reviews on Google My Business, but none on Yelp!, Facebook, or other sites, this could be a cause for the deleted reviews. Simply put, it is not natural and spontaneous if every single customer who reviews you leaves the review on Google. This is a good indicator of spam—or maybe that you over-coach your customers about how to leave a review for your business only on Google.

Although I encourage practices to focus most of their efforts on Google, other review sites, such as Facebook, can be helpful as well. Thus, if you know some of your patients to be active on Facebook, or if your email address on file for a patient is not Gmail, which is the email account associated with an active Google profile, ask them to review you on other sites instead of Google. I will give you more precise tips on how to do this in the strategy section later.

Did the review appear elsewhere on the internet?

It is great that patients love you so much that they want to tell everyone how great you are on multiple sites, but unless the customer writes unique reviews on each review website, you may risk multiple reviews being removed, not just on Google My Business.

If the exact same review appears on Facebook, Yelp!, or on a "testimonials" page on your website in a way that is just copied and pasted by your web designer (rather than set up through a technical integration) it will appear as a duplicate review on your Google My Business page and could be removed.

If your patients love you so much that they want to post on multiple sites, you likely have a close enough relationship to just let them know their review is likely to be removed if they post the same thing on multiple sites, so they should either post a different review or just post on one site.

Was your review written from a location that is too far away from your business location?

Most dentists are likely going to be receiving most reviews locally from patients in the area where the practice is located. Thus, if Google sees reviews from other parts of the country, its spam filters may become alerted. This is why it is especially important for dentists to avoid hiring companies to get reviews.

Do many of your reviews originate from the same online location?

Google can recognize how people get to their website to leave a review. So, if you have a "Leave us a review" page on your website and send all your patients to that page before they leave a review on your Google My Business page, Google may flag your reviews as manufactured. Google likes reviews that appear naturally "in the wild." This is another reason that using software to make it easier for your patients is helpful. When you send your patients an email or a text with a link to provide feedback about their experience at your practice, their email or phone will be the referrer.

Google is also geo-targeting reviews, so it knows exactly where they are being received from. Why do you think when you use Google Maps for directions to a restaurant or another business, you get a review request after you leave the destination? Google does not send you one while you are there, or there might be bias. This is why you do not want too many patients to write reviews while they are in your physical location, regardless if they are using you WiFi or on their own cellular network.

Are you offering incentives for patients to leave reviews?

Do not offer discounts, coupons, or free products to entice patients to leave you a review. If Google notices, you may lose *all* of your reviews, not just the ones you incentivized.

I have been asked many times about running a contest and giving away a prize to anyone who leaves a review during a certain time frame. At best, this is a gray area, so be cautious when and if you do something like this, but I like to teach only best practices and do not believe a review contest is one of them.

What I do recommend is if you want to incentivize anyone, incentivize your team to have a conversation with the patient when they are leaving the practice about receiving a text message asking for feedback about their experience in the office. If they can get their name mentioned in the review, you know the team member has spoken with the patient about it. They deserve an incentive. Nothing wrong with doing it this way, and guess what? It works really well.

The Takeaway

As simple as it sounds, the No. 1 way for practices to use reviews to get found online is to provide an exceptional experience to your patients and ask each of them to leave you feedback in the form of a review.

INDUSTRY INSIGHTS

Positive online reviews are almost as good as personal word-of-mouth recommendations with regard to trustworthiness. In this digital age, online reviews, especially Google reviews, play an essential role in helping your business grow. When customers search for a practice on Google for contact information or for directions, among the first things they see is the Google My Business listing, which includes reviews, the average rating, and the contact information. This means that most of your potential patients who have landed on your Google My Business listing will already be making the decision as to whether to call your practice or not.

In my early days when I began my practice, I was often broke and in debt. Every single patient who came during that time was a lifeline to our business, and marketing was extremely expensive. One time we had a new patient who was the only one on the schedule that day. Fifteen minutes before her appointment, she called and cancelled. I later found out she was on her way to our office, but then she Googled directions and read a negative review about our practice. I was very disappointed, but happy at the same time because she told us the reason why she cancelled. From that experience, I came to the realization that our online reviews are our reputation.

In addition, not even all 5-star reviews are the same. For example, when your business receives a well-written, authentic review from a patient who shares his or her story of positive experiences about you and your team, then it is far more meaningful than 5-star reviews with either no comment or just generalized comments.

In my dental practice, we have treated countless patients who sought treatment with us—including full-mouth smile makeovers, implants and braces—because they read our Google reviews. People tend to relate to other patients' experiences before they make their decisions. This is the reason I always emphasize acquiring well-written, authentic reviews. Well-written reviews that contain stories, personal endorsements, and before-and-after experiences provide the most powerful testimonies about your practice.

Another benefit of having a trove of positive authentic reviews is that it will more than counterbalance any negative reviews that any practice will invariably get over time. Even the most successful dentists know that some patients will never be satisfied with you and your team no matter what you do. Out of our 400-plus Google reviews, we also have a few negative reviews. These are patients whom my team would love to send to some of our competitors! Seriously, these are inevitable, so don't let them affect you. Just focus on taking care of your patients, and ask them to share their experiences. This is not as difficult as it may seem. The key is to bond with your patients and provide a caring, professional experience. Then ask them to share those experiences about your practice and your team. Assure them that their reviews will provide a positive impact and guide other patients who are looking for an exceptional professional experience. The last step is to simplify the process using an innovative review software system, which will save them time and effort in sharing their experiences.

Your online reviews are your reputation advertising your business online, 24/7. The best thing you can do for your business is to ask your satisfied patients to share their positive experiences about your practice with other potential patients. This is the best way to attract new patients, grow your business, and save money on marketing.

—**Dr. Nathan Ho, DDS,** *cofounder and CEO of EnvisionStars,*
a software-as-a-service (SAAS)

Google reviews will be the most valuable, but a mix across other sites will be helpful, especially on a popular site such as Facebook. Yelp! can be frustrating, so I pay little attention to it and encourage many practices to do the same.

Focus on running your business and providing great service and products, then ask your happy patients to provide feedback about their experience. It is also good practice to back up and monitor your reviews, then perform an audit when reviews go missing, but do not lose any sleep over it. The easier thing to do if a review goes missing is to replace it with a new one. Harness the power of your happy patients who want to talk about you but don't know how.

Online Review Exercises

1. In a private browser, run the same Google searches you ran after Chapter 2, namely for "dentist in" and "best dentist in" followed by your city, town, or neighborhood. Take note of the practices that appear in the map results and scan their reviews. Generally speaking, those practices will have at least a few dozen reviews and regularly get new reviews, especially in densely populated areas.

2. If you decide to collect reviews manually, create a document with links where patients can leave you Google My Business and Facebook reviews. Keep this document handy so your team members can email the links to patients to leave reviews.

3. If you decide to use software such as BirdEye to help you collect reviews, schedule a custom one-on-one demo with me to see how they can simplify your process, I'd be honored to talk with you. You can schedule a BirdEye demo with me personally by booking some time on my calendar at drlentau.as.me/birdeye. It is what I do when I am not running my practice. You can also email me at Len@DrLenTau.com or call my cell at (215) 292-2100. Yes, I know it's a strange move for someone to put their cell phone number in a book and invite anyone to call him. But I pride myself on being helpful and responsive. Feel free to call or even text me. If I can't answer right away, I'll call you back as soon as I can.

Part 2

Getting Found in a
Compelling Way

CHAPTER 4

Everything You Need to Know About Your Practice's Website

I cannot emphasize enough how super-important your website is. It's the face of your practice, your online billboard, and your marketing hub. It's where you are going to be sending all of your patients and potential patients to find information about your dental office. But every single year, it seems like the true value of a website decreases as other factors increase.

Websites over the years have changed from being 50 pages deep with tons and tons of content educating patients about the various procedures of your practice to a mini billboard or subway ad designed to grab attention very quickly, contain some basic information, and convince them to call the office.

With so many website companies out there looking to get your business, how do you choose which one to work with? What are some things to look for in a website, and what are the key aspects you need in a website? I work with many website companies that I trust immensely and have done work for myself and my clients. Check out the resources page on DrLenTau.com/BookResources to find a list of trusted vendors.

Local citations and online reviews are much more important when you're getting found because each can push your practice to the top of the search results in a way that is generally within your control. A website, on the other hand, is many times the difference-maker.

A great website can take four to eight weeks or more to develop. Even a basic website takes a couple of weeks, and a two-week website will not be very nice. It might be simple and clean, but it will not add a lot of value beyond serving as an online business card. It will likely only list your services, contact information, and maybe some other basic information. But it will not help you get found. I would personally stay away from companies that create a template website in just a few days. Template websites are known to have duplicate content that does not help you differentiate yourself from an SEO perspective.

Too many dentists spend four to eight weeks and thousands of dollars developing a beautiful website before claiming and optimizing their local citations, setting up a basic social media presence, and beginning to collect online reviews. That can set their practice back for *months*.

Startup practices open their doors without any reviews and spend a ton of money on mailers to let people in their neighborhood know they are opening, but when prospective patients go online to read about the practice and they don't see any online reviews, they simply decide not to come into the office. You need to get reviews *before* spending money marketing your practice. So stop your marketing spend until you have a steady flow of reviews. I just recently spoke to a practice that spent $20,000 dollars on a direct mail campaign and postcard campaign, but the company it hired was more focused on the print media than an online presence. When the mailers and postcards were released, the office had zero—I repeat *zero*—online reviews, and the ROI it got from these campaigns was horrible. The practice lost a ton of money, and after speaking with me, they realized the mistake. Another office that reached out to me six months before opening decided to make reputation its first priority. When it opened, it had 18 Google reviews, which allowed them to have a significantly better ROI on their mailers.

The key is to lay the foundation for getting found as you build or revamp your website. Start claiming and optimizing your citations, building your social media presence, and, most importantly, collecting online reviews as you build or revamp your website. Those are the tools that will help you get found.

Your website is a branding and marketing tool.

From a reputation marketing perspective, your website only needs to do two things. First, although your website can serve many *business* purposes—such as answering common questions or providing forms for people to download to make their visit more expeditious—from a *marketing* perspective, your website is also a branding tool.

That is because patients will almost never type your web address into their browser when looking for a dentist (unless they were personally referred to you). They search Google and other search engines, and your website is very important in that process.

Additionally, people may look at reviews and social media before going to your site, so by the time they get to your site, they have already developed a positive opinion of you from social media and online reviews.

"Reputation is everything when it comes to building a digital brand."

—**Stacey Kehoe**, *Get Online*

If your site is simple, clean, and modern, with conveniences like online scheduling, web chat, and payment processing, people will associate those characteristics with your office and will be more likely to take the next step and make an appointment. You also want to make sure you have photos of the doctor and team, a smile gallery to show the work that you have done, photos of the office, reviews about your practice as well as your contact information.

If your site is old, clunky, and hard to navigate, patients will associate those characteristics with you and will likely move on and choose another dentist who has modern technology.

Second, your website needs to be mobile friendly because more people are searching on mobile. Research shows that 82% of smartphone users use search to find a local business.[11]

With the explosion of mobile browsing, search engines have started to punish websites that are not mobile friendly, pushing them down the search results. Additionally, just like the desktop version of your website tells desktop visitors about you, your mobile site tells mobile visitors about you. Make sure the mobile version of your site represents you how you want to be viewed.

When building a site, here are some of the most common mistakes that I see website companies make. Load up your website, and evaluate your own site to see how many of these mistakes your website company violated.

- The contact information is buried. Are your details listed clearly on the upper right or left side? The name of the practice, address, telephone number, and email address must all be in the upper menu—not in the middle and certainly not in the footer. It's ridiculous how many websites are missing this.

- There isn't a call to action button on every page. Be sure to create an appointment button.

- No doctor and team photos or bios are on the site.

---

11   https://www.thinkwithgoogle.com/marketing-resources/micro-moments/being-there-micromoments-especially-mobile/

- If there are photos, they are clinical photos and images. Think faces and smiles instead—you do not want to gross people out.
- The pages are slow loading—no Flash or animation.
- Testimonials are written by a web designer.
- It has duplicate content or is a template site.
- The site is not taking advantage of branding.
- Navigation is difficult and doesn't make sense.
- There is no onsite blog.

Website trends change, but some important elements include:
- Video—the more the better. Patients are expecting this, whether you have welcome videos or video testimonials. This has become the gold standard, in my opinion. Patients expect to see video on your site.
- Before-and-after photos. We are a very visual society, so show the work that you are doing.
- Social media. It's here to stay. Get involved, and be likeable. With the increasingly popular use of Instagram as a marketing tool, you want not only an Instagram account, but also a button that easily links to your fantastic photos. For a more detailed analysis of your online marketing, please go to DrLenTau.com/dymo and I can send you a report of how you currently look online, and will make suggestions to get better results.

Website Checklist: The Top 10 Must-Haves

1. A great-looking header with a clear, high-quality logo at the top of your website
2. Simple and consistent navigation with relevant pages categorized in suitable submenus
3. An easy-to-find, clickable phone number on all pages

4. An easy-to-find contact form to encourage phone-shy patients to contact you

5. A mobile-responsive design or a separate mobile website

6. Your street address and operating hours on every page

7. A comprehensive "About" section covering the dentist and staff with their professional qualification, photos and bios, vision/mission statements, press coverage, and awards that your dental practice has received

8. High-quality images of the actual office on the main pages, and perhaps a virtual tour with Google Street View

9. Social media buttons and links to your social media profiles (You may also want to include the latest status updates in the footer or sidebar.)

10. A comprehensive contact page that includes a map with directions, including opening and closing hours, public transport routes, amenities available at your office, payment options, new-patient discount information, new-patient forms

For more details and a comprehensive checklist for setting up your website for success, visit the resources page at DrLenTau.com/BookResources. And if you would like me to take a look at your site to give you my impression of what characteristics it displays from a reputation marketing perspective, I would be happy to. Just email me at Len@DrLenTau.com or call my cell at (215) 292-2100.

CHAPTER 5

Using Social Media Effectively

Social media is an important place to show people what makes your dental practice the right one for them. In that sense, although people ask for suggestions and *can* find you through social media, the primary benefit of social media is as a branding and communication tool. It allows you to show the human element of your practice and become what I like to refer to as likeable.

Social media accounts are places for people to engage with you and see how you interact with others. They give people a look into how you communicate with people and how you and your team operate together.

"Your brand name is only as good as your reputation."

—Richard Branson

If your profiles are incomplete and inactive, or if your posts or interactions are rude, it will reflect negatively on your practice. If your profiles are complete, you post regularly, and engage with people in a pleasant way, people will view that as a positive and will be more inclined to do business with you. Social media is not about selling dentistry. You will turn off your audience if you choose to use your platforms to sell your services. As the saying goes, "In a world full of noise, the way you get people to care about you is to care about them first."

On Google, people will initially do a general search for dentists in their location. Local citations and online reviews are the two best ways to organically appear on the first page of results.

When people find you either by Google search or referral from a friend or family member, the next thing they do is search for you specifically. That is when social media and the way you collect and manage online reviews become most important because social media profiles and online review sites are some of the top search results when people search specifically for you or your practice.

In other words, people are more likely to see your social media accounts by searching "Leonard Tau" than "best dentist in Philadelphia." This is why social media is in the "getting found in a compelling way" section and not the section about getting found. Someone will normally find your Facebook page, YouTube videos, and other social media sites on page one of Google when searching for your business.

I was just speaking with a dentist, and he said he did not have a Facebook page for his practice, but that his patients mentioned they were checking in and seeing his Facebook page when they searched his name. Turns out that someone created an "unofficial" Facebook page for his practice which was ranking very high on page one.

Although he did not push out any of his own content to this page, he had 30 likes and 168 check-ins. There were so many comments from happy or raving patients that other patients were coming in based on what people were saying on this page. This is so powerful. You need to know how to reap the benefits of social media. This is social media at its finest.

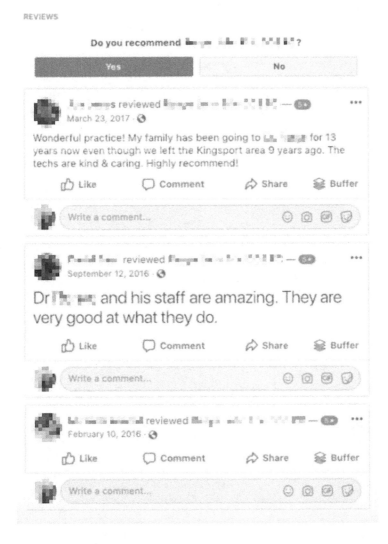

Why Social Media is Important

Social media is important for three reasons. First, it has become a trusted place for potential patients. Patients like to communicate with other patients about their experiences with dentists, just as restaurant visitors or consumer-product customers like to talk about their experiences online. In many ways, social media act similar to reviews, providing a window into being a patient of yours.

Second, more and more patients like to use social media to communicate with you. It's a free way to communicate with people through public broadcasts or private individual messaging in a way that fits into their day-to-day life.

This will become even more important as a greater percentage of adults are growing up using social media as a communication tool. According to a global social media communication study by Smart Insights, 70% of Americans are using social media in 2019, spending more than 70% of their time on Facebook. If people see you offer a Facebook chat option for simple communications or for booking appointments, more and more people are likely to appreciate that. (It can also send a subtle message that your practice keeps on top of the latest technologies in the dental world, too.)

Third, social media can help you control more of the top search results for prospective patients searching specifically for you. A Facebook page with its online reviews feature active is often one of the top search results, for example. Thus, having a professional and active Facebook page with a number of great reviews from your online review strategy can create a strong impression.

How to Use Social Media to Get Found in a Compelling Way

The best way to use social media to get found in a compelling way is to use it to build trust and relationships. Notice I did not say to sell dentistry. That is important.

Although social media *can* be used to sell dentistry, such as by using Facebook ads to make offers to people, that is more of an advertising technique and only works as long as you are paying money for your ads to be shown. Once you stop paying, your ads disappear, and your practice goes back to the way it was.

A stronger and more long-term approach is to utilize social media to build trust and relationships with people who are or will become your patients. That only requires two things: a simple setup and a simple strategy.

Your Simple Social Media Setup and Strategy

To build trust and relationships with the right people, it is important to focus your attention in the right places and have a consistent professional and branded profile that gives people an easy way to get in touch with you. This way, your activities will get you found and make it easy for people to make an appointment once you have built enough trust with them, no selling necessary.

The best places to focus your efforts are sites that Google and other search engines value and where your patients are active. In the dental world, this means focusing your time and attention on YouTube, Facebook, Instagram and, to a lesser extent, Pinterest, Twitter, and blogging activities. Here is why each of these sites or activities is important and a simple strategy for each of them.

YouTube

YouTube is the one of the most important social media sites for two reasons. First, it is not only owned by Google but also ranked highly by Google. It is the second most searched site on the internet, second only to Google itself. Thus, by adding content to YouTube, you are making your content more likely to come up for people who search on the first and second most searched sites on the internet. For example, if you want people to come to you for teeth whitening, creating short videos that answer the most-searched questions about teeth whitening and that show before-and-after images are great ways to move up in the search results.

By building this type of content, your YouTube channel can come up on search results when people run topic-based searches, such as "how teeth whitening works," as well as for your name or your practice name.

Second, video is a powerful visual tool way to build trust with patients. After watching trust-building YouTube videos, patients come in with answers to their most common questions and already knowing, liking, and trusting you. Even better, with YouTube, you can do it once and showcase it over and over again. Finally, YouTube allows users to share and comment on videos, which lets you to engage with them directly.

Some of the most effective trust-building content for YouTube includes giving people a virtual tour of your office, introducing your best team members, answering common questions, and posting video testimonials from happy patients. This is another example of *trustimonials*—sharing videos from community events you host or attend. Share TV appearances, and turn audio interviews into video content by having someone merge the audio file with a background image to create a video file.

We live in a visual world. Video is the present and the future of social media and practice building, and YouTube is at the center of it all. If you could only do one thing on social media, posting videos on YouTube would give you the best bang for your buck.

After creating these videos, you can then embed these videos on your website, your Facebook pages, and other pages as well to increase their visibility.

To show you the power of YouTube, I released a weekly video blog about different topics a few years ago. One of the videos I did was on cracked tooth syndrome, and it was me interacting with a patient who had a cracked tooth, explaining how we can diagnose it and what the treatment options are. When you do a search on Google for cracked tooth in Philadelphia, this video is on page one (see below) and has been viewed almost 16,000 times.

INDUSTRY INSIGHTS

Over the past year, Google has been beta testing the concept of video reviews in its Maps section.

In anticipation of Google allowing videos in its review section, marketers are proactively advising clients to produce video testimonials. (At GPG, we like to call these video trustimonials; thanks to Dr. Len Tau for coining that phrase!)

The first-mover advantage is real. If your practice consistently releases video testimonials now, it will be positioned to capitalize on the release of Google video reviews before most of your competition does.

Though they don't directly impact the reviews portion of Google's search algorithm yet, you can also benefit from using video testimonials right now. Video is a content type that Google gives more ranking credit to than regular text content, so it provides an SEO benefit.

Your video testimonials can even be one of the videos that comes up when a Google search is made—a video search listing.

— **Pete Johnson**, *Get Practice Growth*

Facebook

Facebook is the second-most important social media site for dentists and would be first if it were not for YouTube's search value. Facebook's value from a reputation marketing perspective comes from three things.

First, it is the most active strictly social media site on the internet. Virtually all of your current and future patients use Facebook on a regular basis. If your patients are there, you should be there to build trust with them.

Second, Facebook allows patients to "check in" to your practice to let their Facebook friends know they are in your office and for patients to leave recommendations for your practice. When a friend checks in, it is free advertising for you. Also, recent, regular, and positive recommendations get people into your chair.

Third, Facebook has a strong relationship with Google, too, although not as strong as YouTube because Facebook is more likely to come up when people already know you and search for your name or practice name to check you out before deciding to make an appointment. Thus, a professional-looking business page for your practice with good reviews and quality posts gives you control over one of the higher-ranking search results on Google right when people are deciding whether to make an appointment.

To get started using Facebook, set up a free business profile, post regularly to your timeline, and engage with people. Ask friends, family, and patients to "like" your page, "check in" when they are in your office, and post about their experience. This will help you start building "likes" for your page. Post pictures of reviews people leave on other sites.

Ask people to leave you Facebook recommendations. Post the same types of content you would on your YouTube channel, even reusing your YouTube videos on Facebook. Post pictures of your office, new equipment, team members, and more. If you are not sure what to post, snap a picture in your office, let people know you are looking forward to a great day at the office, and ask what they are looking forward to.

For reputation marketing purposes, you do not have to overcomplicate things. You do not need sophisticated tactics or ad campaigns. You just need a professional profile and an active account with simple content, including images and videos. One of the best things you can do is go "live" on Facebook; your followers may join, and you can interact with them. You can start with an office tour, maybe jumpstart a contest, or just offer some education to your followers.

Instagram

Instagram now has more than 1 billion users, according to Dreamgrow, making it the third most popular social networking app. As researchers write, "That is the answer to the question, 'What will be the next big thing?'"

Once a forum for sharing photos with friends and followers, and browsing through other people's images of travel, food, and myriad other interests, Instagram now has a slightly more serious side. More than 200 million Instagram users visit at least one business profile per day—meaning your practice could get massive exposure through the photo and video app.

The first step for dentists is to create a business profile with the relevant information. Then you can begin filling your feed with photos and videos that showcase your practice. Steer clear of shots that might turn off potential patients; instead, you might share images of staff members having fun, or post a call to action with your phone number and website.

On Instagram, high-quality content, real photos, and responding to followers' requests are important. You want to post regularly (one or two posts per day), but also avoid overposting, which could turn off potential patients. Instagram "stories," which disappear in 24 hours, can entice patients with tutorials and tours of the office among other activities pertaining to your practice. And if you see your practice tagged in somebody else's feed, respond with a comment, which will increase your visibility.

With 90% of Instagram users under the age of 35, it's a great way to attract younger patients.

Pinterest

Pinterest is an online bulletin board that lets you post visual content and engage with people who comment on or share your posts, which the site calls "pins." Pinterest is less known than YouTube or Facebook but has a good search engine influence, and its users are *very* active. Pinterest users regularly share pins they find visually appealing or inspirational. Pinterest is also a place where people click through to websites on a regular basis if they like your image and want to learn more.

This makes it a great place to post before-and-after images, inspirational or aspirational imagery, fun quotes, beautiful images of your office or team, or images that link to your YouTube videos or website where you answer questions people want answered.

Again, simplicity is the best approach with Pinterest. There's no need to create additional content for Pinterest, however it is a great and fast-growing place to share content and has also built a strong relationship with Google. As it grows, that relationship will only get stronger.

Pinterest, founded in 2010, is a surprisingly popular social media channel. According to a Feb 2019 survey:

- Pinterest has 250 million users every month.
- Pinterest has reached 83% of U.S. women aged 25 to 54. This is a huge target for the dental profession. This segment of the population are often referred to as the "deciders" as they control 80% of household spending.
- 50% of new signups in 2018 were men.
- 34% of Americans aged 18–49 use Pinterest.
- High-income and well-educated U.S. households are twice as likely to use Pinterest compared to low-income and less-educated households.

In my opinion, your Pinterest roadmap should be to extend the reach of your dental website to new pockets within your target market, elevate your brand appeal and online reputation, and eventually boost your search engine rankings as Google indexes Pinterest images quite often.

Twitter

Twitter is a very active social media channel where you can share short text posts, images, or videos with people. Although it is not as useful as YouTube, Facebook, or Pinterest, it has a few features that make it a valuable social channel for reputation marketing.

The most effective use of Twitter is to share reviews, communicate with patients, comment on and engage with strategic partners such as local businesses you would like to build a relationship with, and fill last-minute openings. I have personally tweeted that I had a last-minute opening, and the first person that took the spot would get a 20% discount on the visit. Ten minutes later, the appointment was booked.

A lot of people are on Twitter, which is both a good thing and a bad thing. The timeline moves fast, so your posts will not have a long shelf life, although people who click on your profile can scroll through all of your posts.

Thus, it is not a place I encourage people to spend a *lot* of time, but it is a popular site with a lot of people there, so using it as a branding, communication, and networking tool is worthwhile.

Blogging

Like YouTube, blogging is not often viewed as traditional social media, but it is a valuable tool in your reputation marketing arsenal. Blogging helps you inform conversations people are having and get noticed by Google and other search engines. In other words, even if nobody is coming to your blog, the search engines will see your site as active and relevant to the topics you are writing about. Thus, when people search for a topic you are writing about, your site will be more likely to come up on the search results.

As with the other social media techniques, the best part about blogging is that it is a long-term strategy, unlike paid advertising, which goes away when you stop paying. You can post answers to questions people are asking, discuss new technologies in the dental world, and position your practice as one that is involved in the latest ways to improve patient care.

Use the same strategy as YouTube when it comes to choosing what to write about. You can even embed your YouTube videos into a blog post and write an article about the same topic. Write lists, such as "5 Ways to

Whiten Your Teeth," do product reviews like "The Best Toothpaste for Sensitive Teeth," or offer tutorials.

You can turn all of your preparation or care instructions you give to patients after their treatments into blog posts, too. Once you have written your post, add an image with the title of the post that you can use to share your post on your social media channels. This will let you share the blog post on your social channels in a way that will get noticed and help continue the conversation.

If you have a website company posting blog posts for you as part of their social media strategy, please make sure the content is unique to your practice as a blog post that is repeated many times by multiple practices has zero search engine effect. If you have a custom blog, search engines will love your content.

Simple Social Media Exercises

Social media is an important tool to getting found in a compelling way because Google and other search engines value them, and your patients are active there. With reputation marketing, simple is truly good enough. These three steps are all you need to get started.

- First, you need to set up a professional-looking profile on each channel or add a blog page to your website.
- Second, create content on a regular basis. If you have trouble searching for topics, answer questions that people ask you on a regular basis or start with topics I mentioned here. It is also best to create a content calendar at the beginning of a month to make it easier to find things to post.
- Third, distribute the content on every channel, and engage with people who comment on, "like," or share your posts. Do not worry about sophisticated ad campaigns or complicated strategies.

This three-step process will make your accounts stronger than the vast majority out there and help you build trust and relationships with current and future patients. It is that simple.

Take a few minutes to look at your social media channels. Are your profiles consistent and professional? If not, update each of them so they are. Are you creating content on a regular basis?

If not, try creating five posts in the next ten minutes. Keep them simple using the tips in this chapter. Then share them on your profiles once a day for the next five days. As you go through the day, look for things that would be interesting to share. Keep track of them in a notebook or your phone. Then sit down to schedule them once a day. These exercises will help you get into a content-creating mode.

Are you engaging with people who comment on, "like," or share your posts? Take a few minutes each day to look at your accounts and go back to thank people or answer questions.

CHAPTER 6

Building Your Five-Star Reputation

I n Part 1, we talked about how online reviews can help you get found online. That is important because we know how many people search Google to find a dentist. But the impact of reviews on compelling people to make appointments with you is even more important than how they help you get found.

The reality is, you can *pay* to get your practice listed on the first page of Google search results by advertising with Google. It can be expensive and risky, and I do not recommend it as a long-term solution to marketing your practice, which is best accomplished with search engine optimization. But you technically *can* get to the first page of Google by advertising with them.

Social proof is the tendency to see an action as more appropriate when others are doing it.

—**Robert Cialdini, Ph.D.,** *Influence:*
The Psychology of Persuasion

One thing money *cannot* buy is the ability to get people to actually call and make an appointment with you. You might get people to click on your ad to check you out, but most of them will search for reviews about you before making an appointment. This is the reason that I don't recommend starting with Google Ads or even Facebook advertising using funnels until you have a significant number of reviews.

A better plan is to be proactive in building and marketing your five-star reputation so you do not need to rely on paid advertisement. That can get expensive, and I recommend paid advertising only if you are looking to promote a specific high-revenue procedure, such as Invisalign, cosmetic makeovers, teeth whitening, or dental implants. I recently spoke with an office that was spending $100 dollars a day on Google Ads for its startup practice, and it had five reviews and 3.8 stars. They were basically advertising their bad reputation. What a waste of money.

Other practices spent money on paid advertising, especially Google Ads, placing ads that would show up when people were doing an exact Google search for their practice name. With the right online presence in place, you should not have to do that. Your name and Google My Business profile should appear right at the top of the page. This is a very common mistake many practices commit when running paid advertising campaigns on their own or if they hire the wrong dental marketing company.

If you want to run paid advertising, it's a better idea to have your office name be listed as a "negative keyword" in most cases. Negative keywords prevent your ads from running when people search those keywords. Because you will almost always appear as the top organic result when people search for your practice name, having your ad show up on that particular search could result in your paying for clicks (if people click your ad) made by people who would have clicked your website or Google My Business listing anyhow. Other negative keywords you might want to include in your ad campaign include terms such as "affordable dentistry," "free dentistry," or any other terms you do not want people associating with your business.

A much more effective—and cost-effective—option for getting dozens of new patients every month is to become more personal in the review process (see below) and build a five-star reputation that people find organically. In this chapter, we'll talk about how you can do that.

INDUSTRY INSIGHTS

As a marketing strategist, I have had many experiences where the power of reviews has blown me and my clients way. A few years ago, I was working as a dental hygienist in a pediatric dental practice in a highly competitive area. I always made a point to ask every new patient, "How did you hear about this practice?" It was important to all of us to understand how families were choosing this practice for their children.

One day, I had a new patient who came in with his dad. Per my usual protocol, I welcomed them to the practice, gave a tour, discussed medical and dental health, and then in conversation started to ask why they chose this particular practice. The dad then told me something interesting—he said, "Actually, my wife wanted to go to your competition's location—they take our insurance, they're closer to our home and have decent reviews."

I said, "So why us?" He then told me that on Google, he saw one major differentiating factor that separated us from the competition—our practice was replying to all the reviews. He said that because of the personal replies back to each review, he knew that he wanted to bring his children to a practice that did not just "ask for reviews" but cared to read feedback and acknowledge it.

If a practice takes that much time for their online presence, imagine how much effort they put in when it comes to seeing patients in the office—they must care and are invested in the well-being of the patient. When I think about this encounter now, it makes me think about how much of who we are as a practice can reflect by how we take care of our patients online. Reviews are not a "trend" or an "SEO tactic." They are ways to show off your practice culture from all angles.

—Minal Sampat, BA, RDH, *dental consultant*

First, we'll discuss how to earn a five-star reputation. That involves building a practice that patients will readily and honestly rave about online. Second, we'll talk about how to turn that patient success into *social proof* that compels people to take action.

With a five-star reputation and social proof, you will not just appear on the first page of search results; you will also appear in a way that gets people to actually pick up the phone and make an appointment with you.

Turning Raving Patients into Social Proof

In 1962, the television show *Candid Camera* demonstrated the power of social proof by sending a group of actors into an elevator with one "victim." The goal for the prank was to see whether the actions of the group would affect the actions of the victim.

The show focused on three victims. With each victim, actors entered the elevator with only one other person—the victim—inside. Instead of turning to face the front of the elevator, the actors remained facing the rear.

In each scene, the victim eventually turned to face the rear way, too. The first victim did so gradually, as if he was just casually shifting around. The second victim hesitated momentarily but then quickly spun around.

The third victim took conformity to a whole other level. In that scene, three men and one woman joined the young male victim. After they entered, all four actors spun to face the rear. Unlike the other two victims, the young man quickly followed suit and spun around as the door closed. When the door reopens, all five occupants are facing to the left. The three actors are all holding hats in their hand. The young man is wearing the hat he had been wearing the whole time.

Before the door closes again, the four actors spin to their left again to face forward. Almost without delay, the young man conforms. The next time the door opens, all five occupants are seen completing another spin to face backward again. They then all spin to face forward.

The scene then cuts to one of the actors wearing and then removing the hat he had been holding earlier in the scene. The two other male actors are seen holding their hats. It is unclear from the show clip whether those actors had been wearing their hats or removed them before the third actor removed his hat. The clip only shows the third man removing his hat and the other two holding theirs. As soon as the third actor removed his hat, the victim followed and removed his hat, too.

As the scene ends, all three male actors put their hats back on. Can you guess what the victim did? That is right. He conformed.

In each case, the behavior of the actors became social proof of the right way to behave in the elevator, and the victim conformed.

So how does this relate to you? It is *exactly* what happens with online reviews, only in digital form as *social proof.*

Social Proof and Dental Marketing

For years, businesses have used social proof to get people to change their behavior. For example, in the 1950s, businessman Ray Kroc added the phrase "Over 1 Million Served" to the sign for the first McDonald's franchise he purchased. As McDonald's grew, he updated the sign to "5 million," "400 million," "1 billion," "19 billion," and more.

We all have opinions about McDonald's food, good and bad. But they have *social proof* that they have served billions of people and display that fact prominently on their signs.

That message essentially tells people "Millions (or billions) of people have eaten here. We must be doing something right." That is social proof.

What your practice listing looks like on Google's search results is your version of social proof. What does your listing prove? Does it prove you have a five-star reputation and many happy patients? Does it prove you are behind the times or not easy to work with?

Online reviews are your version of "billions served." If you have three reviews, your "sign" will not be very compelling. If you have dozens of recent reviews from happy patients, your "sign" will get people to take action.

Let's revisit the process that potential patients go through when searching for a dentist on Google. Remember, when people search Google for a dentist in their area, Google shows paid ads, followed by a map with three or four listings, followed by organic results on the first page. If you search for "best dentist" and your city or town, you are likely to see three or four dentists on the map.

Let's assume the four listings have the following reviews:

- 88 reviews, 3.9/5 average rating
- 9 reviews, 5/5 average rating
- 25 reviews, 4.2/5 average rating
- 78 reviews, 4.8/5 average rating

If you put yourself in the shoes of an unknown searcher, which one would you click on first? Most people tend to click on the listing with the best social proof, which is measured mostly by the "most, best, and recent" reviews.

In this case, that is most likely to be the one with 78 reviews and a 4.8/5 average rating, assuming many of the reviews occurred in the last couple months. The one with the most reviews overall has a significantly lower average rating. The one with 25 reviews has fewer and lower ratings. The one with nine reviews does not have enough reviews to carry much weight.

Thus, the one with 78 reviews has the best social proof. That will cause searchers to click on the listing and look at the reviews. If some of the reviews are recent (ideally in the last two weeks) and appear real, they will likely call that dentist to ask about their insurance or make an appointment. Remember that most patients using Google to search for a dentist online don't have insurance since those usually go to their insurance company's website to see who takes their plan. They may then look you up to see what others say. They might never click on the other three dentists.

A client came to me recently for help collecting social proof. At the time, he had only two Google reviews. He had 11 Facebook reviews but only two on Google. If they searched for him by name, the results included two Google reviews and links to a bunch of pages on his website. That is not what you want to happen when people search for you.

Contrast this dentist with what people see when they search for me on Google. The first page of search results when people search for me by name includes about 228 Google reviews as of this writing, reviews on other sites, and lots of other positive information outside of my website. That gets people's attention.

If you are not building your 5-star reputation with social proof, you can be assured your competitors are. This is not optional anymore. Consumers *trust* social proof. Studies show they trust it 12 times more than product manufacturers' descriptions, which includes the business's websites.

This is why more and more patients are making decisions right when they are reading your reviews, without actually even going to your website. They trust your website much less since most dentists only share their positive reviews on their website. Do you have any negative reviews on your website? I do, and this makes me more credible in the eyes of a potential patient.

Consumers view business-generated content as more biased than consumer-generated content. It is the same for dentists as it is when shopping online. People trust customer reviews more than they trust content created by the businesses selling the products. That includes product descriptions, marketing messages, and statements on the company's website. It does not matter how many times the company says "high quality," if the reviews say "low quality," people will not buy.

In the dental world, your website can describe you as talented, friendly, or caring. If you have no reviews or have reviews that say otherwise, patients will not believe you. Get your patients talking about you online, in a positive way, and you will start earning more and more patients.

In the offline world, leveraging the power of positive patient testimonials is called word-of-mouth marketing. It is simple. When you treat people well, they will refer you to their friends and family.

In the online world, I call the power of positive patient testimonials word-of-*mouse* marketing. Word-of-*mouse* marketing is even more powerful than word-of-*mouth* marketing in two important ways. First, positive online reviews last forever. Second, positive online reviews impact not only people your patients know. Complete strangers will see their words and trust you to be their dentist.

Building a Five-Star Reputation to Grow Your Practice

I cannot overemphasize how important this step is to reputation marketing. Before you can market a five-star reputation, you need to build a practice that *earns* a five-star reputation.

If your practice *deserves* a five-star reputation, it will be much easier to collect and market a steady flow of authentic positive reviews, which we'll talk about in the next section. So, if your practice does not treat patients like VIPs, the first step to collecting positive reviews *must* be to look inward at what you can do to start deserving better patients.

Dr. Anissa Holmes, who wrote the foreword to this book, calls this *Delivering WOW*. Anissa treats every patient to a spa-like VIP experience in her practice. She offers free gourmet coffee and pastries. She lends patients iPads and headphones to use during their visits. She gives patients warm towels and had her team trained in hand-and-arm massage techniques to make patients look forward to going to the dentist.

Anissa and her patients go out of their way to make sure patients leave thinking "*WOW*" about their experience, and it shows in the reviews of her practice. For example, here is what one patient who visited her office for a free consultation said on a Google review:

> I went in for a free consultation based on a promotion they had, but at no point was I left feeling like I had not paid. I was greeted by name shortly after arriving, given a tour of the facility, and introduced to pretty much every employee that was present. I was nervous about the visit but was comforted by the well-trained staff.
>
> My dentist and the dental hygienist who started my process were both very gentle and thorough. They explained all my options and answered all my questions. I am definitely going back!
>
> —Shanna-Kay

As you can tell from this review, Anissa and her team work hard to address the top concerns of patients. The office does not make people feel rushed or unwelcome even if they come in for a free service. Instead, Anissa's team members took the time to give this patient a tour of the office, introduce her to their staff, conduct a "thorough" consultation, explain her options, and answer questions. They were gentle, friendly, and came across as "well-trained." They comforted this patient, who described herself as going in "nervous."

Now imagine asking a patient who just had that type of experience if they would mind sharing their experience through an online review. They will be much more likely to review the practice than if the experience was nothing special. Patients will talk about their experiences when they are extraordinarily good or extraordinarily bad, and you would much rather have them talking about those great experiences.

When you treat patients well, you will not be limited to getting reviews from your best and most loyal patients. You will be able to generate a steady flow of motivated and *raving* patients who will gladly leave you an honest five-star review. Anissa and her team *earn* their five-star reviews better than almost any practice I know by treating their patients to that *WOW* experience.

If you want help earning reviews, visit the resources page at DrLenTau.com/BookResources. There you will find links to several resources for creating five-star patient experiences. Be sure to also subscribe to my *Raving Patients* podcast, where I interview experts about how to build a profitable practice that earns a five-star reputation with its patients.

I also highly recommend reading Anissa's book, *Delivering WOW: How Dentists Can Build a Fascinating Brand and Achieve More While Working Less* and listening to her podcast by the same name. (I also talk about turning patients into raving fans on my *Raving Patients* podcast.)

Building Your Five-Star Reputation Exercises

1. Visit the resources page (DrLenTau.com/BookResources). Pick up a copy of Anissa's book, *Delivering WOW: How Dentists Can Build a Fascinating Brand and Achieve More While Working Less*. As you read through it, use the strategies she shares to set yourself up to *earn* five-star reviews.

2. Subscribe to my *Raving Patients* podcast, and listen to the first episode where I talk about why this is so important and introduce the concept of earning quality reviews.

3. Take a look at your current reviews. Do they tell a story? Are they recent? Think about how they could be improved.

4. Talk with your team about how important it is to earn five-star reviews by treating patients like VIPs. Let them know about your dedication to continuous improvement, and solicit feedback from them about how you can improve patient experience. They will see things you do not. Their input can be priceless.

5. If you do get some negative reviews, do you see a pattern? Are they about a specific team member, waiting issues, or billing issues? If you see multiple negative reviews about the same problem, you need to fix it. When you address your patients' concerns, you have an opportunity to turn your critics into your raving patients.

Part 3

Collecting and *Marketing* Reviews from Raving Patients

CHAPTER 7

Best Practices for Online Review Management

I talk with thousands of dentists a year at dozens of conferences where I train dentists to build five-star reputations. Every time I speak, I ask people what they do to collect reviews. The vast majority of dentists say, "Nothing."

Well, if you do nothing, you will get nothing. Remember, if you do the same thing you have to expect the same results. If you want different results, you have to consider different behaviors. Asking for reviews is simple if you and your team know how to handle the process.

INDUSTRY INSIGHTS

What separates practices that get good reviews from those who don't get many, or worse, any reviews?

I can tell you exactly what the differences are. I'm lucky enough to speak to literally hundreds of dental professionals every year during my speaking engagements. At every presentation, I ask my seminar attendees to raise their hand if they do these:

- Ask their patients for reviews all of the time.
- Ask their patients for reviews some of the time.
- Don't ask their patients for reviews at all.

Whether it's an audience of 300 or 30, the breakdown of the answers is generally always the same:

- 1/3 of people who respond ask their patients for reviews all of the time.
- 1/3 of people who respond ask their patients for reviews some of the time.
- 1/3 of people who respond don't ask their patients for reviews at all.

There are distinct differences between these dental teams. Check them out and see which group applies (or that you'd like to apply) to your practice:

GROUP 1

These teams ask patients for reviews **all of the time**. They often have dozens or hundreds of reviews on the most important review platforms—Google reviews and Facebook.

These teams are usually confident and open to share what makes them successful. Their number-one reason for success is systems. They have well-oiled processes in their practice, and their team members are well informed about them. The team has a clear understanding of their review goals, what they are trying to achieve, and why it's important. They know exactly what tools or methods they can use to grow their reviews, and they implement and follow through to keep their good reviews growing month after month.

GROUP 2

These teams ask for reviews **some of the time**. Like Group 1, they have solid systems in place to generate reviews, but they take things one step further by vetting who they ask for reviews and not. These teams like to take a more personalized approach.

For example, they may only ask patients for reviews when the patient pays them a compliment. They may have systems in place to alert them when a Google Gmail user is coming into the office so they can take advantage of the opportunity to ask that patient for a Google review. These teams are also often sensitive to how often they reach out to patients for reviews—they don't want to "pester" patients and want to make sure that each team member is aware of who is asking for reviews, and when, so they don't appear too aggressive in their review invitations.

Like Group 1, these teams may role play how to invite patients to share their reviews so they are comfortable having these conversations. They may even pay attention to nuances in their language. One practice told me they never ask for reviews, only for testimonials. They felt asking for testimonials alluded to leaving only positive reviews.

GROUP 3

These teams have several reasons for **not asking for reviews at all**. In some cases, teams say they didn't even know that asking for reviews was important. Some teams say they know generating reviews is important, but they don't know how.

Again, these practices discover value in learning about the proven tools and options available to them—many of which you are finding here in this book.

—**Rita Zamora,** *Dentistry Social Media Expert*

While patients may know how important reviews are, many of them will not think to leave you a review if you do not ask—and ask them in the right way.

That is true of almost all patients. Even most patients who find you from reviews will not leave a review until you ask them.

I get it. You are busy. Your staff is busy. And you do not want to annoy your patients. I do not want you to annoy people, either. And I do not want you to add more work on your staff or yourself.

So, the key to collecting reviews is to do so in a way that does not take long, does not annoy patients, and helps you attract more of the right patients for your practice so you can spend less time (and money) on marketing.

In other words, collecting reviews the right way can actually *save* you time and money in the present while making you more money in the future. When you collect reviews the right way, life will become *easier* for you and your team.

In fact, I have eliminated all paid advertising except for some Google Ads and Facebook sales funnels campaigns specifically targeting Invisalign, smile makeover, and implant patients in Philadelphia. I know dentists who spend *thousands* of dollars a month on paid advertising plus countless hours planning and managing those ad campaigns.

I eliminated all but some well-managed Google Ads and Facebook ads for those high-cost procedures because I collect reviews the right way.

Here are the exact steps you can take to collect reviews the right way. As you are reading this, be aware that all of this can either be done manually or using software such as BirdEye (or another company listed in the Introduction) to save even more time and ensure consistency.

One thing about BirdEye. I am a big fan of automating as much as you can. But no reputation marketing *software* is the solution to your marketing challenges itself. The reputation marketing *process* is your solution.

So, just as I did with local citations and even social media, I am going to walk you through every step so you can understand exactly what the process is and do it all manually if you want. If you prefer to get help simplifying the process and getting more consistent results, softwares like BirdEye, Swell CX, or even Podium can help. I am not here to sell software, though. If you are interested in having help, you can review a demo of how BirdEye works or even schedule a free personalized demonstration by going to DrLenTau.as.me/birdeye.

I also included a bonus section on the resources page that compares different software options for you. This is important. Many software providers claim to help with reviews when they are really just communication software, not reputation marketing software. Others help collect reviews and don't help market them. Still others help with local citations but not reviews. True reputation marketing software helps optimize your local citations, automatically request and collect reviews, and then market those reviews through multiple channels, including a dedicated microsite, on social media, and on your website.

Step 1: Make sure your team knows what makes a positive review, a good review for reputation marketing purposes.

If you treat your patients like VIPs, they likely have a lot of great things they can say about you. And if you ask them to leave a review the right way, they will likely be happy to do so.

But they *still* might not know what to say in their review, however. I will explain how to ask for reviews the right way to make sure patients are leaving the most helpful reviews possible for reputation marketing purposes.

Which of these two reviews do you think would be more valuable?
- A review that says "Dr. Tau is the best!!!!" or
- A review that says "The staff at Pennsylvania Center for Dental Excellence could not be friendlier. I am a new patient and I have 'dental phobia.' Dr. Tau is very patient and gentle. A true perfectionist. I am glad that I found him and his staff, and I could not be happier."

The second one will perform much better, every time. (It is also an actual review of my practice.) While "Dr. Tau is the best" is very high praise, the second one comes across as more authentic. It tells a story. It also contains more detailed unique content about to be indexed on Google and shared on other social media channels, an important part of a good reputation marketing plan. Stories have an impact on people; they can connect emotionally, which leads them to make purchasing decisions.

I encourage my clients to share public reviews on social media with a message that says something like, "We love our patients and are honored when we receive positive feedback on our internal forms. One of our patients left us written feedback saying we exceeded her expectations today. Thank you! That's our goal for every patient!"

Reviews that include no narrative or only say something like "Dr. Tau is great!" "The best dentist in Philadelphia" or "Great visit, as usual" can be helpful for the star ratings and SEO, but they are not the types of reviews that will paint a picture for future patients. They can also come across as fake. Finally, they do not give you content worth repurposing on social media or your website.

The best reviews include at least two or three sentences that describe the patient's positive experience. In Step 2, we'll talk about how to generate these types of reviews on a regular basis.

In reviewing a lot of Google My Business pages for dentists, I've noticed that some offices get a ton of reviews on Google that have only star ratings no written review. This has very little effect on ranking. If you are one of those offices, you need to change the way you are asking or use a different software program. I also see a lot of practices with reviews on sites such as Rate A Biz, Patient Connect, Solution Reach, Doctible, and other places that lack the credibility of Google.

Step 2: Ask. But do not ask for reviews. Ask for feedback.

What do you say to patients when you are done with their procedure? What does your front-desk clerk ask them on their way out?

If you are like most practices, you say something to the effect of, "You are all set. See Sam at the front desk, and she will take care of you from here. Have a good day." Your front-desk person probably tells the patient how much they owe and asks how they want to pay if they have not yet paid or helps them schedule their next appointment.

Do not do this. Switching immediately to a monetary transaction as soon as you are done with the procedure kills the positive energy you worked so hard to earn. Instead, ask patients about their experience at your office.

When you complete the procedure, ask patients if they were comfortable. Ask how they are feeling. For cosmetic procedures, remind them of the positive impact the procedure will have on their life, such as "You can be confident with your gorgeous smile." For implants, say, "You will not need your dentures anymore" or "You can eat whatever you want again."

Have your front-desk staff ask, "How was your experience today?" instead of going straight for payment methods. For cosmetic procedures, have them ask if the patient is excited about their new smile. These two or three questions will build rapport and get the patient thinking about all the positive things about their appointment.

When the patient is done talking about their great experience, have your team say something like, "We love to hear that. We are always looking for feedback. Later today, you will get a text message and email asking you about your experience today. We read all responses. Our team loves to hear what our patients like best about coming here so we can do even more of that."

Actual verbiage that I recommend is: "Thanks for coming in today. We hope you had a great experience and want to tell others about it. Just so you know, you may be getting a text message asking for feedback and we look forward to hearing what you have to say."

Asking for feedback at the end of an appointment is a much better experience for your patient than going straight to asking for payment. It is also a much better way to ease into a conversation about leaving a review. Feel free to add your own flavor to how you ask, but asking for feedback makes the conversation much easier for your team as well. Asking for a review just sounds odd.

If you have provided a great service and make it easy for your patients to provide feedback, they will normally oblige and write a great review on Google.

Step 3: Follow up with the patient that same day with the link to leave you a review on Google.

People live busy lives. If you only waited for people to leave before asking for a review, you would never get any. The conversation in Step 2 lays the groundwork for you to actually get people to review your practice.

Even with that groundwork, only a small percentage of people who say they will leave you a review will actually do so, often less than 5%. That is okay. You don't need more than that to benefit from reviews if you ask enough people, but many times, the team becomes frustrated at the percentage of people doing it or are tasked with other things that take their attention to something else within your practice. Even a steady flow of a few reviews a week can help. But with a 5% follow-through rate, asking every patient about their experience and getting permission to follow up with them is so important.

Here are some other effective ways of getting more reviews.

Before people leave, you could hand them a card or sheet with instructions for leaving a review. That will increase your conversion rate slightly by acting as a reminder and making the process easier.

Emailing a link for people to leave a review is much more effective because they do not have to type anything but their review. You could also include the text of what they wrote on the form in your office as a reminder and suggest they can copy and paste it to make it easier. Some practices have a link in their signature asking for a review as well. I have seen this have limited success similar to placing a link on your website taking them to a place to write their review.

Texting the review link is even more effective than an email. People's email inboxes are full of promotions and spam. Thus, your email might end up in a spam filter and never make it to their inbox. Even if it makes it to their inbox, only a small percentage of business email is opened. Think about how many unread emails you have compared to how many unread text messages. If you are like most people, you have dozens, hundreds, or even thousands of unread emails but fewer than five unread text messages. I have personally seen some of my patients' cell phones with more than 135,000 unread emails. Sending them an email is a pointless exercise. Texting them is the key to standing out and getting noticed.

Here's a screenshot from someone in the audience at one of my conferences. Look at the number of unopen emails they had (the second app from the bottom in the first column). They had more than 425,000 unopened emails! Now look at the number of unread texts (the second app from the left on the bottom row): *Zero.*

While that's an extreme example, your patients are the same. Your best odds of actually getting a review are to follow up by text later that day when they are no longer in your office. I do not recommend getting reviews while the patient is in the office.

I have seen numerous issues with patients connecting to free WiFi that you may not be offering but a neighbor is. Multiple reviews coming from the same IP address can flag the review, which Google may take down. Google also does not want you to necessarily get the review in the office because of bias or pressure the patients feel with someone hovering over them. As I mentioned earlier, why do you think that when you use Google Maps, Google does not send you a review request until you have left the place of business? Google is now geo-targeting reviews and knows exactly where patients are leaving them.

I recently talked with a periodontist who thought she had more than 100 Google reviews. It turned out she had fewer than 50, and most of the recent ones she had gotten were taken down because they were left in her place of business. She was using a service from a well-known marketing company, so please be aware of the terms and conditions of collecting reviews before you try something that may backfire.

Stick with Google. It is by far the most important review site for most practices. But there are more than 100 sites that collect and publish patient reviews, including Facebook, Yahoo! Local, Bing Local, Rate MDs, Yelp! HealthGrades, and more. Some sites will be completely irrelevant to your practice in your area. Others will have a minimal impact. Google and Facebook are likely to have the most impact on the most practices.

Visit my resources page at DrLenTau.com for a comprehensive list of sites that collect and publish reviews to see what other sites you may wish to target.

The Dark Side of Reviews: What *Not* to Do

By this point, most dentists agree that reviews are *powerful*. As with most good things, though, if you take it too far, it can often backfire.

Thus, before we talk about how to automate your reputation marketing process, I need to warn you of a few things.

First, do not try to *control* what your patients can say online. Your patients have every right to post reviews, good or bad. Do not try to change that. That can backfire, reputationally or even legally.

For example, one dentist had her patients sign a privacy agreement that said her practice owned copyrights to online reviews. The idea behind something like that was for the practice to be able to take down negative reviews or sue for copyright infringement. This practice even fined a patient for a negative review, which was permitted under the privacy agreement that the patient signed.

You may realize that patients sign things many times without even reading what they are signing. An example would be your cancellation policy and the fact that you charge a broken appointment fee. Rarely, if ever, do patients read that there is a charge, so they get irate when you let them know.

Needless to say, this dentist's strategy to own copyrights to online reviews backfired big-time. When word gets out—and it *will* get out, especially in today's social media world—people from around the world will bombard your listing sites with negative reviews. Your online reputation will be destroyed.

This has happened countless other times. I shake my head in disbelief when I see it happen or see a dentist recommending legal action in a post about it in the various Facebook groups that I am part of. Worst advice ever.

If you take it further and actually sue a patient, it will be all over the internet and cause you even worse press. When a Manhattan physician sued a patient, asking for $1 million after a negative Yelp! review, the story made national news.

If you focus instead on earning positive reviews, implementing a simple reputation marketing plan like the one I have outlined in this book, and treating negative reviews like I suggest in the next chapter, you will not even need to worry about that.

Second, never, **ever** pay for reviews. It is deceptive, obvious, and does not work. Google can tell and will take them down. And anyone who knows anything about reviews can spot them. You will end up with the same reviews from different people. You will have reviews from overlapping names. You will get reviews in bunches. It is a waste of time and money and can make you look bad.

On the same note, do not offer incentives to a patient to write a review by offering them something in return for a positive review. This practice is very much against the terms and conditions of Google and Yelp! (An incentive is anything that can be construed as value.) Yelp! has a blog that points out businesses that have violated such terms and conditions, and they have penalized businesses for offering items from a whitening pen to credits on the account and even tickets to Disneyland.

Third, focus on having an average star rating between 4.5 and 4.9. I mentioned this before, but it warrants highlighting here. Although you cannot completely control your star rating on Google or Yelp!, you can on some other sites, especially if you are using good reputation marketing software.

For example, BirdEye allows you to redistribute reviews you get on one site to others. It also allows you to filter those reviews by star rating before redistributing. While it might be tempting to only redistribute 5-star ratings, it will make it look fake, especially if your Google rating is only 4.6. Include some negative ones for redistribution so your overall rating is below a 5. Those negative reviews make the positives look more credible. On my website (Philadelphiapa.Dentist), I actually list some 3-star reviews for credibility, and many times patients have mentioned that they had never seen that before, but they now trusted my reviews more.

Fourth, do not get reviews from nonpatients. Google sees the location of the review and compares it to the location of your practice. If too many are coming from too far away, it will likely end up rejecting the reviews. If the review somehow makes it through, it will likely be an ineffective "Dr. Tau is the best!" type of review or obvious that the person never went to your practice. It is just not a good idea. It is also against review site terms of service and can get you delisted.

Fifth, although I do recommend using software to make your reputation marketing easier, I do not recommend paying to advertise or have a premium listing on review sites. Sites such as YellowPages. com, Healthgrades, or even Yelp! have premium profiles that you can purchase, which they claim will get you more traffic. It is not that they are trying to scam you. It is just that I do not see it as a good use of your money, and ones that have tried it have been seeing poor results.

You can do everything you need to earn and collect reviews for your practice for free. You can collect feedback in your office for free. You can text or email for free. You can follow up with patients for free. You can claim profiles on review sites, such as Google My Business, Yelp!, or Healthgrades, for free. You can collect reviews on the review sites for free.

There's also no truth to the rumors that if you advertise on a review site such as Yelp!, it will filter in more of your positive reviews and filter out more of your negative reviews. That has never been proven, and I do not believe it to be true.

Yelp! just has a very secret and complicated algorithm to try to capture authentic reviews from accounts they trust. If your patient has never left a Yelp! review and leaves you one from your waiting room, Yelp!'s algorithm will likely filter it out.

From Yelp!'s perspective, that type of review would be unreliable. It could be your hygienist setting up an account to leave a fake review. It could be a patient sitting with you looking over their shoulder at what they are typing. On the other hand, if a patient who has left 25 reviews over the past year leaves you a review from their home, Yelp! will be more likely to let it through, positive or negative. It does not matter whether you advertise with Yelp!.

YELP! IS NOT A BULLY—HOW YELP!'S RECOMMENDATION SOFTWARE WORKS

With nearly 200 million reviews and more than 175 million visitors every month, Yelp! is far too important to ignore in many parts of the country. Yet, it continues to be a source of frustration and anxiety for many business owners and dentists in particular. For years, the company has been accused of extortion as thousands of business owners claim that Yelp! filters out positive reviews when the owners decline to pay for advertising. Although Yelp! has always vehemently denied that reviews are manipulated to force business owners to advertise, the accusations—and anecdotes by frustrated business owners—have never gone away.

It's natural to become upset when a positive, authentic review from a real patient disappears into the "not-recommended" part of Yelp!. It's even more upsetting when a bunch of reviews gets wiped out at once whenever Yelp!'s recommendation software is updated. And, it looks suspicious when it coincidentally happens right after we refuse to buy ads or even pick up the phone when the Yelp! representative calls.

The truth is that many practice owners become frustrated because they do not understand how Yelp!'s recommendation software works. This recommendation software is designed to showcase the most reliable reviews and move less trusted reviews into a "not currently recommended" section of Yelp!.

The reviews in this section are not gone but are hidden, and do not affect the overall business rating. It's also important to understand that Yelp!'s recommendation software algorithm is automated. It affects both positive and negative reviews and treats advertisers and non-advertisers the same.

The way the algorithm works is it looks at many different signs to evaluate whether a review is "reliable" or trustworthy, including review quality, user reliability, and user activity on Yelp!.

According to Yelp!, every review is automatically evaluated for usefulness based on quality, reliability, and user activity. Some reviews get filtered out, while nearly 75% of all positive and negative reviews are deemed reliable. These are well-written, detailed reviews shared by people who are known to Yelp! because they have a completed profile, have multiple friends on Yelp!, and are active users of Yelp!, whether they post reviews frequently or not. Reviews from Yelpers who contribute frequently are particularly sticky—they tend to pass the recommendation software as Yelp! is promoting reviews from users who share their rich and detailed experiences regularly. But even reviews from those who don't post often can be sticky if the reviewer uses Yelp! frequently by logging into an app, booking appointments, liking or complementing other reviews, or checking into a business on Yelp!.

So, while it can be extremely frustrating to see genuine positive reviews from real patients disappear, keep in mind that the recommendation software is fluid. There are many reasons why a review may end up in a Currently Not Recommended section of Yelp!. These might be reviews from new users, users with incomplete profiles and few friends, or those who haven't engaged on Yelp! regularly. Any of these things can easily change. Once a user becomes more engaged and active on Yelp!, their reviews can move into the Recommended section.

Despite the frustrations, Yelp! offers many ways for dentists to interact with patients and potential patients. A successful strategy on Yelp! does not require spending any money and is an opportunity to positively represent your practice online, get found, and get more patients through your doors.

One of the ways I recommend to try to get more Yelp! reviews to stay in the recommended section is to use the check-in feature. You *are* able to offer an incentive (such as an $10 office credit or a Starbucks gift card) to a patient to check in at your office. A check-in creates more visibility for your practice, and also triggers a review request from Yelp! for even more visibility. I have recommended this to many practices, which have seen much higher Yelp! success rates with this strategy.

The same is true for sites with free and paid accounts. Whether you pay to upgrade an account does not impact your reviews. I suggest sticking with free accounts.

Also, avoid anyone who tells you they can pay to collect reviews or get negative ones removed. They cannot. If they somehow manage to do something in the short term, it is likely against terms of service and will end up hurting you in the long run.

The best practice is to stick to free accounts and use steps one through three to earn and collect real reviews. The only things I ever suggest paying for are convenience and consistency when it comes to reputation marketing. You can get that with good reputation marketing software.

Sixth, make sure you know and follow the rules of the review sites. If you follow the basic principles of earning reviews and use good reputation marketing software, you are likely in pretty good shape. But it is still good practice to know the rules so you do not end up doing anything on your end that gets you to lose reviews or get your account delisted, such as having a review terminal in your office. You used to be able to do that. Not anymore.

How to Automate Your Reputation Marketing

If the idea of sending emails and texts with links to the relevant review sites seems like a pain, I get it. When I started collecting reviews for my practice, there was no simple and effective way to make the process smoother. We could keep review links and sample text or email language in files to copy and paste, but we needed to do most things manually. And there was no great way to keep our listings consistent.

Not only that, but the rules set by Google and other sites changed so frequently that practices got penalized and permanently lost reviews they worked hard to get. They also saw reviews disappear seemingly without explanation. If you do not keep up, it is hard to know what to do.

For example (as I mentioned earlier in this book) Google decided to remove many older reviews that were labeled "A Google User." Overnight, practices lost a number of reviews and had no idea why, especially ones that had been collecting reviews for a while. I lost almost 50 Google reviews overnight. I went from 235 Google reviews to 177. Here's why. I was one of the original people who got involved with reviews back in 2008, before Google+ existed. When Google+ came about, everybody created Google+ accounts with names. Before then, people's reviews were anonymous, only referring to the reviewer as "A Google User."

Many years later, Google decided those anonymous "Google User" reviews were not credible. So, immediately, anybody who had been a longtime reviewer or an early adopter of reviews, as I was, lost a lot of reviews. Because I had a direct line to what was going on behind the scenes, I understood this was another way of Google telling people it wants fresh, current, relevant reviews, rather than older reviews. But that was some pretty hot news that broke in 2018.

Another significant rule change in 2018 happened when Google no longer allowed companies to use software to engage in what they call "review gating." Basically, review gating happens when practices give patients a prescreening question such as, "Did you have a good experience?" Or, "Would you recommend us with a thumbs up or thumbs down?" before getting a review from them. Many dentists used software to ask patients if they had a positive experience. If they pressed *yes*, they would get a follow-up message asking them for a review. Many reputation marketing and practice management software programs allowed practices to do that. It was very common in the industry. Google then shut down that process.

If you managed review collection manually by copying and pasting into texts or emails or used practice-management software to send requests using a "review gate," you needed to know about the change and manually update your process. If you had good reputation marketing software to help, the change took place automatically behind the scenes to keep you compliant. There are still companies that do review gating, so make sure you are compliant, or you could risk removal of some if not all of your reviews.

Manual processes have no way to keep up with the rules as they change. You need to constantly monitor the updates on top of managing your practice. That comes at a big expense in terms of your time or your team's time—which you are paying dearly for.

Fortunately, we have come a long way since I created iSocialReviews, and you do not have to invent your own software program to solve that problem anymore.

Quality reputation marketing software can help you for a few hundred dollars a month. The good ones keep up with the latest changes and update their software to help you comply with the rules. They also communicate with you when things change so you do not end up losing reviews.

That happened in 2018, when all the big changes in Google's review algorithm caused a lot of dentists to lose reviews. Many of those reviews were lost forever for practices who collected them manually or used software that did not have the same reputation for respecting the rules as BirdEye does.

So how do you find the right software? I am not going to just say to pick BirdEye, although I do believe strongly in it. I would rather show you the different options (such as the list in the Introduction) and help you make an informed decision. Afterward, I will discuss the various options available to you in addition to BirdEye and what makes them different and at the same time unique.

Finding True Reputation Marketing Software

The first step to effective automation is choosing software that automates more than just the review generation process and at the same time sends the reviews to Google or Facebook directly. (Just as an FYI, third party software is no longer able to send Yelp! as a choice.)

When comparing these products, I will separate them into two categories: reputation marketing software and patient communication software. Many practice management or patient communication software products can send emails or even text messages reminding your patients about their appointment or that they are overdue for their six-month recurring visit. But they are not as effective in generating reviews as they place them on their own microsite in most cases. Or, even worse, they are just internal reviews that nobody ever sees. Sure, you can program them to send review requests and reminders. But that does not make them reputation marketing software. Good reputation marketing software does much more than just collect reviews and communicate with patients.

Here are questions to ask yourself when evaluating software. Visit the resources page at DrLenTau.com for a detailed comparison of BirdEye and other software solutions so you can have the best information available at your fingertips if you choose to automate.

1. Does the software help you manage your local citations and online presence?

Reputation marketing software must scan how your business appears online and ensure your online citations are consistent on the most important sites. The best reputation marketing software would also sync videos, photos, hours of operations, and other content across the most important listings in the dental market.

This helps you create a broad, consistent presence online to help you start showing up on the Google Map results when people search for dentists in your area, as we discussed in Chapter 2.

2. Does the software make it easy for you to get new reviews on top review sites?

The best reputation marketing software helps you get reviews online and offline, integrates with your practice management software, and works by sending text messages, multimedia messages, and emails. It lets people review on whatever device they have and sends the reviews directly to the most important review sites. The software should also be customizable so you can include your logo and your own message to your patients that is consistent with what your team is trained to say when requesting a review.

This is important to make it as easy as possible to collect reviews and get them *everywhere* they can add value to your practice.

3. Does the software help you monitor and respond to reviews without having to visit and sign into dozens of review sites?

Monitoring reviews is an important step in reputation marketing. While I do not recommend responding to all reviews, especially negative ones, which we'll talk about in the next chapter, being able to monitor what people are saying about you online is critical to reputation marketing.

Reputation marketing software should alert you when people post reviews online and allow you to respond from one centralized location. It should also allow you to flag reviews as spam, slanderous, or in violation of review site terms and conditions.

BirdEye takes this very seriously, allowing businesses to respond directly to customer feedback from all sites using one centralized dashboard. We also send real-time new review alerts via SMS or email to relevant employees so management can take action on customer feedback and address problems before they escalate.

4. Does the software automate review *marketing*?

Review marketing is much more than just collecting and monitoring reviews. That is why review marketing automatically repurposes your online reviews to take advantage of that free, patient-generated and free content about you and your practice.

For example, BirdEye creates a personalized website—known as a microsite in online marketing terms—for each practice location. That microsite is optimized for SEO and indexed by Google. It includes reviews, your hours, services, and contact information.

This creates a powerful presence that often quickly shoots up to the first page of Google results when people search for your practice. It's important because it allows you to control two of the roughly 10 spots on the first page instead of just one. It can even help push something negative to the second page, where hardly anyone visits.

I tell people your website should take up no more than two spaces on the first page of Google search results for review marketing purposes. The rest should be review sites full of positive reviews. A personalized microsite that is included with your automation software is an easy way to start building a powerful first page presence on Google.

In addition to a microsite, review marketing software should allow you to automatically promote positive customer feedback on social media, review sites, and company websites. This way, people can see all the great things patients have to say about you even when they are not searching for you on Google. BirdEye automatically or manually allows you to promote your best reviews to Facebook as a post and Twitter as a tweet and give your coding to show off your great reputation on your actual website.

Make sure your software does not only collect reviews. It will severely limit the value you get from those reviews.

5. Does the software allow you to **control** your public presence from a centralized dashboard?

Communication and review-collection software allow you to send messages to patients and collect reviews in return. But they do not give you any real level of control over what happens to negative reviews.

In BirdEye and other true reputation marketing software programs, you can filter what reviews are used in your review marketing automation. For example, I recommend practices work to maintain between a 4.5-star and a 4.9-star reputation online. This makes a positive impression and avoids appearing fake by having a perfect reputation.

But that does not mean you want to plaster your microsite with 1-star reviews, especially if they are inaccurate. And while you cannot control whether the 1-star reviews appear on the site where the patient left the review, you can control which reviews get added to your personalized microsite, promoted on your website, or distributed to Facebook and other review sites.

With a few clicks of the mouse, you can set it so only 3-star reviews and above get used in your reputation marketing campaigns.

6. Does the software monitor social media?

True reputation marketing software does not only monitor your reviews. It also monitors what is being said about your company on social media and allows you to respond directly from one centralized place.

For example, BirdEye allows users to monitor social media commentary in real time, identify conversations about their practice, and even participate in the conversations from its dashboard.

You can select keywords to monitor, such as your name, your practice name, and even dental keywords. It then aggregates all relevant conversations into one dashboard.

7. Does the software integrate with your practice management software?

A good rule of thumb is if your practice-management software *is* your review software, it is not true reputation marketing software.

But good reputation marketing software integrates with your practice management software to help you automate everything. For example, BirdEye integrates with most practice management software including Dentrix, easydental, curvedental, Dolphin, eaglesoft, Planet DDS, Opendental, SoftDent, WinOMS, and many more.

That allows our clients to have their feedback requests automatically sent out at the end of the day. Your team only has to let patients know they will be getting the feedback requests and that the team is looking forward to reading it.

It is important that you can control how those requests are sent out, too. By default, BirdEye will not send more than one feedback request every 30 days. That way, if someone comes in for a cleaning and comes back for a filling a week later, they only get one request. You can adjust that time frame if you want, but this helps you automate without worrying about annoying your patients.

8. Does the software make it easy for you to measure and track results?

If your software does not let you track your progress with detailed reports of reviews, ratings, and customer sentiment over time, by location, and by source, you are at a big disadvantage. As with most marketing campaigns, your best results come from testing and adjusting your strategies based on the results.

That allows you to focus more time and energy on the things that are working and adjust things that need improvement. It can tell you one location of a multilocation practice needs to be retrained or reminded to ask patients to leave feedback. It gives you important insights into all aspects of your reputation marketing plan.

BirdEye, for example, gives you several ways to measure your return on investment, including with traffic reports of website visitors and leads.

9. Does the software allow you to communicate with your patients and potential patients easily?

One of the most common requests I get is for a way to communicate with patients through our robust platform. Offices want to communicate not only with their existing patients but also with website visitors who may become patients of the practice. Most reputation marketing software products already have contact data for your patients that they pull from the practice management software. With BirdEye, you can two-way text your patients as well as include the newest feature, which adds a chat button to your website to allow you to interact with your visitors.

A number of different reputation marketing software programs are available, such as Podium and Swell CX, just to name a couple. They all collect reviews and make it easy for your patients to get them to Google and Facebook. All are very good services but not as robust as the BirdEye platform.

Comparing these reputation marketing platforms to what I will refer to as communication software, I want to use an analogy that I think most dentists will understand. The communication software platforms on the market are like a general dentist—they do a lot of things including confirming appointments, reminding your patients if they are overdue for their recurring appointment, sending campaigns such as year-end insurance reminders, reactivating patients who have not been in the office for a couple of years, two-way texting your patients, treatment plan follow-ups and, of course, review generation.

But because they do so many things, they are not great at doing everything. They're like the "jack of all trades, master of none." When it comes to reviews, most companies generate reviews that go on their microsite and require multiple steps to get the reviews on Google or Facebook. Some make the dental practice see the review before the patient can post it, and some just put a link in an email that sends the patient to Google. The programs in this category include Revenuewell (which I currently use), Lighthouse 360 (which I've used in the past), Demand Force (which I used before Lighthouse 360), Solution Reach, Yapi, Legwork, and a newer product that has what it takes to compete with the big boys: Modento.

Revenuewell gets most of its reviews on a site called patientconnect365; Lighthouse users will notice most of their reviews end up on RateABiz; Demandforce sends most reviews to their Demandforce microsite; and Solution Reach will add most of their reviews to Smile Reminder (it has recently changed its site to Solution Reach). If you use one of these products, I am sure you know what I am talking about. The only other places these reviews may show up are on your website and possibly on Facebook, but the only ones who see those are your existing patients or people who already know who you are.

The other platform I want to mention is Weave, which I would place into its own category. I also use Weave in my practice. It is a VOIP phone system that also serves as a two-way text messaging product and communication software. Weave has also added fax capabilities and has a very good review generation software as well.

The moral of this story is that for most practices that want to make reputation marketing an important part of their marketing plan, they are going to need both reputation software and communication software.

For a more detailed description of these platforms please check out the resources page of this book at DrLenTau.com/BookResources.

Are you *earning* and *marketing* your five-star reputation?

Online reviews are powerful. Collecting them is important. But reputation marketing is about much more than just *collecting* reviews. In fact, collecting reviews is not even the most important part of a good reputation marketing plan.

Before you can collect reviews, you need to *earn* the reviews. And after you collect the reviews, you should harness the true power of those reviews by sending them to your website, social media, and even a microsite.

While you can do all of that manually using copy and paste and taking the time to visit multiple sites on a regular basis, good reputation marketing can help you get better data, results, and returns on your investment of time and money.

For those reasons, I often recommend investing in quality reputation marketing software like BirdEye. Obviously, I am biased in favor of BirdEye. After all, I run its dental vertical. So, I am clearly biased.

But I also know the work and care that goes into making sure BirdEye gives dentists everything they need to collect and market reviews while staying in compliance with the terms of service of hundreds of review websites. That is on top of all the other benefits like maintaining consistency of your local citations from one dashboard.

I have been with BirdEye through many algorithm changes and have witnessed how quickly it adapts the software when rules change. I can attest to the value of quality reputation marketing software that keeps its finger on the pulse of the market.

Reputation Marketing Exercises

1. Because this chapter discusses the main process of collecting and marketing your practice, I have created a checklist of everything you need to do to implement true reputation marketing in your practice. Remember, education without implementation is just entertainment. Go to the resources page (DrLenTau.com/BookResources), and download the checklist for this chapter.

2. While you are on the resources page, take a look at the software comparisons and consider whether you are interested in automating your reputation marketing or prefer to do whatever you can do manually.

3. If you choose to do what you can manually, start preparing the language your team can use to call or text patients for reviews plus instructions to repurpose your reviews.

4. If you prefer having help and want a personalized demo of BirdEye, email me at Len@DrLenTau.com or call my cell at (215) 292-2100. I would be happy to walk you through how

BirdEye can help you. You can also schedule a demo directly by visiting drlentau.as.me/birdeye

5. No matter which way you choose, talk with your team about asking patients for feedback and letting them know you read and value feedback. Let them know about how reputation marketing can help everyone in the practice build a stronger practice while delivering even better experiences to patients. That will help get everyone on the same page with your vision.

CHAPTER 8

Handling Negative Reviews

You do everything right. You've claimed and optimized your local citations. You create an incredible patient experience. You treat patients like the VIPs they are. You ask patients about their experience and tell them to expect a feedback request and that you read every one of them.

Months later, reviews start coming in, and you rise up in Google's search results, first to the map and eventually to the first page for dentists in your area. When people search for you or your practice by name, your website comes up, but the rest of the first page of Google is full of review sites full of four-and five-star reviews and patients *raving* about how great it is to be your patient.

And then it happens. Someone leaves you a dreaded one-star review.

Maybe you have not focused much on collecting reviews yet, but among the handful that trickled in on their own is a one-star review. It sticks out like a sore thumb, and you just *know* when people search for you on Google, that negative review will give them pause.

Or maybe you do everything right, treat patients like VIPs, and someone still leaves a negative review. Many times, they are not even your fault. A patient might have assumed you accepted their insurance

179

and get upset when you tell them your practice is fee for service. Or, a patient might have responded to an ad for a procedure they do not qualify for. Or maybe someone misunderstood something about your treatment plan and feel like you tried to rip them off. And maybe you did do something that made the negative review deserved. Even worse, someone who is not your patient posted something negative about your practice online. You think it is the end of the world, but it is not.

"It takes many good deeds to build a good reputation, and only one bad one to lose it."

—Ben Franklin

Every single day, I get a call, text, or email from a dentist around the country alerting me to the fact that he or she got a bad review: What to do about it? It is always the same story, they don't recognize the patient, the review is not describing the actual experience, it was from a former employee who has an axe to grind, or they just don't want to believe that their practice can receive a negative review.

I have something to tell everyone who is reading this. It is going to happen to you at some point, and unfortunately, there is not a whole lot you can do about it. Google generally does not take reviews down unless they contain hateful, violent, or inappropriate content, contains advertising or spam, are off topic or contain conflicts of interest. Many of the reasons I mentioned above to do not fall into this category and thus Google refuses to take down most negative reviews, no matter how hard you beg and plead. I had a review written by a patient who claimed I was homophobic, which was not true in any way shape or form, and I was able to get Google to remove it, but other than that, I have not had much luck in getting reviews taken down.

If you happen to get a negative Yelp! review, you may get lucky and have Yelp! determine that the review is not trustworthy and send it to the not-recommended section. Otherwise, trying to convince Yelp! that review is fake, from an ex-employee or from a non-patient is nearly impossible as well.

INDUSTRY INSIGHTS

At our offices, online reviews aren't just a business strategy: They are *the* business strategy.

When you put that much weight on customer satisfaction, a couple of things happen:

- Your team works hard to get people to write great glowing reviews.
- Bad reviews hit you where it hurts (think a kick to the groin, only worse).

We've had thousands of great reviews and celebrated together! We've also had dozens of bad reviews that left me questioning whether my own mother still loved me. It's become such a thing that the nerve endings in my right thigh know the specific iPhone vibration attached to a Yelp! review notification. And, perhaps like PTSD, that vibration sends a direct signal to the panic centers of my brain.

Literally, I know immediately I have a Yelp! notification just from my silent phone vibration in my pocket. Over the years, it's gotten easier, and our strategies to deal with online haters have helped me respond better and even boosted our practice performance online (Yes, I've learned that bad reviews *can* be good if we respond the right way.).

Still, there are several reviews I will never forget.

THE GOOD:

> *"Make sure you check out the Viking that works the front desk. He's like a Norse God or something. The interior is like a magical wonderland and makes you feel like you aren't in a dentist's office at all. This place is aggressively hipster, and I love it."*
>
> —Facebook

> *"Holy crap! I love going to the dentist! I never thought I'd say this. Ever."*
>
> —Yelp!

> "When gingivitis and plaque come a-knocking, this doctor keeps the dental chair rocking. Prepare to be orally fixated with Dr. Robin Bethell, DDS, a newbie to Austin."
>
> —Austin Woman Magazine June 2013.

THE BAD:

> *"Dr. Bethell has refunded me the amount I paid out-of-pocket originally for the procedure (about half the total cost of the procedure). I am updating this review to reflect and acknowledge that he has done that. He offered to pay my new dentist the entire amount to fix the tooth, but on the condition that I remove this review. I considered his offer, and have decided to decline. I am leaving my review at "1-star" level, because I still do not trust him and I still believe his true motive is protecting his business, not doing the right thing. If it was the latter, it would not have taken over a year and a bad Yelp! review to get my money back. Again,*

when this incident first happened I needed the entire amount as my old insurance would not pay anything for a 2nd crown. So if I had received my "out-of-pocket" refund a year ago, it would not have fixed my tooth, which is why I requested the full procedure amount refund from Dr. Bethell originally."

—Eliott P, Yelp!

This review taught me the most important lesson ever: Do not challenge angry consumers online. I had gone back and forth with Elliott for weeks, all in the public space. I gave him his money back. I was consumed by this for more than six months. It's absolutely maddening what he did, but what is worse is how I responded. I will never *ever* do it again.

"I brought my son here about a year ago because I saw they are a pediatric dentist. This might have changed over the course of a year, but my first red flag was NO CHANGING TABLE IN THE RESTROOM! Really?? You want me to pretend to care about my child, but want me to change his diaper on the floor. Not cool."

—Marisa P

I still get teased about this one. Immediately after we got the review, I bought and photographed a brand new baby changing room table and put it up on our Yelp! page. "We have a changing table!" I responded. My team laughed and saw how pathetic I was. It was disingenuous and pathetic. I didn't have a changing table, and I should have apologized and owned up to it. Better to have poop on your floor than egg on your face.

THE UGLY:

Without getting into the gory details (most of which you can still read in my one-star reviews), I'll just share that a woman attempted to extort me through Yelp!, and I found out she was doing the same thing to other dentists in the area. We immediately shared stories, and discussed our black-ops mission of revenge. Just kidding—we did nothing and took it on the chin like responsible business owners should.

Over the years and after amassing more 5-star Yelp! reviews than any in the U.S., I've come to these conclusions:

- You learn more from bad reviews then you do from good ones.
- People read bad reviews and how you respond. It is an awesome opportunity to show your humility and tell your story.
- If you aren't getting bad reviews, board complaints, lawyer letters, you aren't working hard enough.

—Robin Bethell, *Forest Family Dentistry*

A pediatric practice had an issue with a patient posting 20 to 30 fake reviews basically saying the same thing, and even though I flagged the reviews, they were not taken down.

Please understand that no matter how well you treat your patients, getting a negative review is bound to happen; you just need to know what to do when you get one.

Here is what to know (and do) when the inevitable negative review comes through.

Do not panic.

It is natural to be upset when someone leaves you a one-star review. But even if it ruins your breakfast to wake up to a one-star review, do not let it spoil your lunch. Do not carry the emotions through the day. That could only be bad for business. Go about your day with the goal of treating every patient with the same VIP treatment they deserve. You may end up getting a positive review before the end of the day to brighten it.

Here is an example of what I am talking about. I received a scathing review from a patient on Facebook in December of 2018.

I started going to PA Center for Dental Excellence years ago when I saw them listed for Invisalign. Before purchasing the Groupon I went in to the office for a consultation because I wanted to make sure it was legitimate.

I was pressure saled into buying the Groupon deal directly with Dr. Tau instead of through the website. He Then he tried to overcharge me for things that were included with the Groupon. Shady.

Throughout the course of my Invisalign he tried to sell me on his overpriced work that I could not afford so I opted to go to my regular dentist. He would say things like well they don't do the work right, or cleanings, etc. He basically likes to claim no other dentist does legitimate dental work except him and tries to use scare tactics to make you pay his overpriced services.

This last visit of mine was the straw that broke the camels back. I have good dental insurance through work that Dr Tau works with. I had 4 cavities that I knew about. I called to ask them what would be my out of pocket expense. I understand that it can't be an exact number so I said over estimate please. I was quoted $300. Fast forward to half my face being numb and Dr. Tau getting ready to do fillings I'm told it's going to be $900. So I said oh no I can't afford that - Taus response because he's money hungry - do you have care credit? Um sure let me go into credit card debt so you can afford $100k cars. 🙄. Nope. Not willing to do that. Let's see a break down because that is insane WITH INSURANCE. The smallest possible cavity at this office costs $250 with the majority of them costing $300-$400. I've called 5 dentist in Philadelphia and Bucks County who've told me that is way too much. When I said that I found that number to be extreme with insurance I was, told I was dismissed from the dental office. I was crying, stressed out and had a half numb face.

Dr. Tau is an opportunistic, scam artist who uses scare tactics and pressure selling to drive his business. I found him to be extremely overpriced and highly unethical. The Hippocratic oath means nothing to this man.

I would highly recommend staying far away from this dental practice.

When I got the notification that I received this review, I was obviously upset as I do not want patients feeling that way about me. I discussed it with my team to avoid issues like this in the future, and at the end of the day, I got this review on Google from a patient who also happens to be a dentist.

What a difference of emotions when you have such a terrible review, and then you end the day with some positive feedback from your patients.

Remember, negative reviews can be a good thing because they reinforce the genuine nature of your four- and five-star reviews. In fact, most of the time, the negative effect of the review comes down to how you respond.

Do not overreact.

In 2016, a New York dentist sued at least four patients for defamation after they posted negative reviews on Yelp! His lawsuit claimed the reviews were unfair and harmed his practice. Can you guess what happened next? If you guessed that news of the lawsuit went viral, including on the popular website Buzzfeed, and then that Yelp! added a warning to consumers on that dentist's Yelp! page with a *link* to the Buzzfeed story about the lawsuit, you would be right.

To this day, before Yelp! allows visitors to read reviews from this dentist, they have to acknowledge that they read a warning, which looks like this:

Consumer Alert: Questionable Legal Threats

This business may have tried to abuse the legal system in an effort to stifle free speech, for example through legal threats or contractual gag clauses. As a reminder, reviewers who share their experiences have a First Amendment right to express their opinions on Yelp.

More information about the action that led to this Consumer Alert is available here.

Got it, thanks!

Image Credit: Yelp!

The only way to dismiss the warning is to click the button that reads "Got it, thanks."

There's no little "x" to click to dismiss the notice. You cannot hit the Escape key and make it go away. You need to acknowledge that you have read the warning by clicking a button right on the warning itself. And, the last word of the warning, "here," links to a Buzzfeed story titled "Yelp!'s Warning: This Dentist Might Sue You For Posting A Negative Review." More information about the action that led to this Consumer Alert is available on the resources page.

That means it is likely that whoever searches for that dentist and lands on their Yelp! page will read all about how the dentist sued patients who posted negative reviews.

You think that makes the genuine four- and five-star reviews seem legitimate? Look, we all make mistakes. And we can all learn from our mistakes, so I will not shame him by mentioning him by name or posting a link to the Yelp! page or his practice.

But what do you think caused more harm to his practice in the long run, the four negative reviews, or the fallout from his response?

The bigger issue in my mind is that Yelp! never takes down the inflammatory words that permanently reside on his Yelp! page for all visitors to see. Think before you do something stupid that can have a lasting negative effect on your practice.

This is just one example of why you should not overreact when someone leaves a negative review, and the funny part is that the review the patient left was not even that bad. Here is the review that he sued the patient about. Note that the doctor's name is redacted. It's not necessary to include the name to make my point:

> ▓▓▓▓▓ was curt and dismissive, and seemed annoyed with the way I answered his questions. But he did seem to be genuinely interested in finding out what was causing my pain, and how it can be helped. However, it was an absurdly long wait. After about an HOUR, I was finally seen (my appt was at 11AM). Then after speaking with him for about 5-10 minutes, he left me for "just a second" to deal with another patient... I didn't see him for another half hour. Of the total TWO HOURS FIFTEEN MINUTES I was there, I think I was speaking to ▓▓▓▓▓ for about 30 minutes of that whole time. The rest was spent in his chair, without being offered a water or a magazine. And at the end of it all, he couldn't help determine what was bothering me. I left with a mouth full of pain and a recommendation to see my dentist for a possible cavity.

Do not respond.

This piece of advice often gets a pretty strong reaction from people. We are human. We spent hundreds of thousands of dollars on dental school and poured thousands of hours into building your practice. We work hard to treat people well and give only the best dental care to patients.

And then someone posts a negative review about you. Fair or unfair, responding is often the *worst* thing you can do.

For one thing, responding to reviews could land you in hot water under HIPAA. For example, one dentist mentioned a patient's "clenching and grinding habit" in response to a comment about an alleged unnecessary tooth extraction. They also mentioned the tooth at issue was not the first molar tooth the patient lost due to a fractured root and said this was the same issue.

By mentioning the patient's clenching and grinding habit, history of losing teeth and fractured roots, and diagnosis of a fractured root for this tooth, the dentist committed multiple HIPAA violations.

When you do respond, you give the reviewer the opportunity to re-respond and then a war of words can ensue online, and it may not turn out well.

Here is an example of what occurred when a dentist in Hawaii responded to a negative review.

First, here's the review:

⭐⭐⭐⭐⭐ 2/11/2013

That was the worst experience I had ever had at any dentist.

The practice called me to ask what to do about it, and I recommended no response since there was nothing specific written in the review. Also, I wanted them to see if Yelp! would push it down to the not-recommended section since this person had zero friends and only four reviews. If the dentist responded, that would have validated the review and made it more likely that the review would *not* be taken down.

The practice insisted on responding. Here was their response:

7/23/2013 · Of course, it is not easy to know that any client of ours was not satisfied with the service we provided. In most cases it is just a simple misunderstanding and our office will immediately correct it. We do apologize that you did not agree with our diagnosis and felt that we were unsympathetic. That being said, our office is known for providing the highest level of uncompromising care to every one of our clients. We look for long-term solutions that will last and prevent people from frequently returning to the dentist. I want to assure you that it was not our intent to be insensitive to your feelings. We hope that you have found a reputable dentist that will provide you with the best care. Read less

This response was apologetic, which I always recommend if you are going to respond to a review online, but it allowed the reviewer to then re-respond in an update to her post, which turned that one-liner into a novel.

Here's part 1:

Update:
The reason why I decided to update my review was that ▪️▪️▪️ dentist keeps on bothering me by sending me unpleasant messages after my last review. Who wants to go back to the dentist who gave you the worst experience ever? I've never gotten confused with ▪️▪️▪️ ▪️▪️. Honestly, I was not completely satisfied with ▪️▪️ but still they were much better compared with ▪️▪️▪️. ▪️▪️▪️ dentist also sent me a message after my not good review but it was more professional and did not bother me at all.

Okay, this is what I had experienced at ▪️▪️▪️. ▪️▪️▪️ told me that I needed unnecessary treatments. She also gave me so many negative and "MEAN" comments which surprised me and scared me a lot. I was almost crying.

She told me it was "TOO LATE" to fix my teeth without getting bridges and implants!
I did not agreed with her right away. Then she kept on telling me how bad my teeth were.

When I was going to ▌ ▀▀, no dentists there had never told me I needed any bridges nor implants. All they had told me was I needed new crowns for my teeth. I thought I should make more research before I spend thousands of dollar for my new crowns. Then I saw very good reviews of ▬▬ ▪ ▄▄ on Yelp and decided to give it a try. It ended up wasting my time and money though.

Anyhow, can you imagine how much I was surprised to hear Dr ▀▀▀▀▀▀ opinion?
If Dr. ▄▀▄▄▄ ▀ was right, it means the dentists at ▄▀▀ did not examine my teeth right.

So, I went to see other dentists right away to find out if everything ▐▌ ▀▀▀▀▀▀ told me was true. One was a well known experienced dentist who was my friend's husband(I did not go see him in the beginning because his office was too far for me to visit regularly). I did not tell him about my visit at the ▀ ▀▄▄ ▄▀ and had him to take a look at my teeth. He said "You need to put some crowns." I asked him if I need to get bridges and implants. He laughed and said "No need. They are not that bad. Who said that?" I told him it was Dr. ▀▄▄▀▄▀▄▀▄ Seems like a popular well skilled dentist according to her website and Yelp. He said he did not know her at all.

Here's part 2:

I talked with many people and I found another dentist near my house and went to see him. He told me the same as my friend's husband had said. All I needed was new crowns. They would do fine. I asked him if I should get bridges and implants. He was surprised and took a good look at my X-ray pictures again and then took another good look at my teeth again and said with a smile, "Crowns would work fine. You don't need bridges nor implants." He told me he did not know why some other dentist told me that I needed bridges and implants. He also explained me why he thought so very well.

Did I need to believe what ▄▀ ▀▄▙▄▜▄█ told me? I still do not think so. She explained me thoroughly. She was the only one who told me crowns would never work out and I needed to spend more than $15,000 to get "unnecessary" bridges and implants.

Again, Dr. ▙▄ ▄▀ ▄▀▄ told me there was no way I could be fine with crowns with so many reasons. She told me every dentist would tell me the same when I asked her an alternated plan. I almost believed her words 100%.

As I mentioned, no one agreed with her opinion at the end. I got new crowns at the last dentist I visited months ago. The bill I got there was around $900 per tooth. Just in case, I asked ▄▄▄ ▄▄▙▄▀ ▄ office for the estimate for my crown and it came out around $1400 per tooth. I got the same material for my crown. There is no problem. I am doing great.

FYI, I also got estimates for my treatment from the ▄▙ ▀ ▄▀▄ and two other dentists. '▀▄ ▄▀▄▙ ▌ ▌ estimates were 20 to 60% more expensive than others for the same treatment with the same materials. I don't believe this difference of the cost is for her skills nor knowledge. I am so happy that I did not trust her and got the third opinions.

And here's the final part:

> I checked other people's review and found out the person who kept on sending me messages was Dr ▪▪ ▪ ▪▪▪▪▪▪ ▪ husband. Please stop bugging me.
>
> All the other staffs there were very nice. The hygienist was good and friendly. The receptionists there were also very nice, well organized and knew what they were doing. I think all those people and the nice building make the office look good. Sorry to say but not the dentist.
>
> I read other people's review and was surprised to hear the dentist was very nice? I guess as long as you obey her opinion without any hesitation, she can be nice to you.
>
> My dentist friend used to told me that you always should get the third opinion before you get any treatment. I did not take it serious but now I understand why he told me so.

This ended up backfiring on the office, and to this day, the interchange is still very visible on the dentist's Yelp! page. If you choose to respond, and some certainly will, please be careful on how you handle the situation. My recommendation is to avoid such online interactions.

Take the conversation offline.

Instead of responding immediately to the review, I suggest reaching out to patients offline. Give them a call, message them, text them—just try to contact them in some way to hear them out and avoid a public showdown. If some of their complaint is fair, let them know that, apologize, and tell them how you are going to use it to improve patient experiences moving forward. Then ask them how you can make things right with them.

When someone leaves me a negative review I believe is unfair, I will always *personally* call them to talk with them directly. Many times, it turns out the issue is merely a misunderstanding. By calling them, you can turn a negative into a positive.

Sometimes patients will edit, respond, or post a follow-up review letting people know it was all a misunderstanding, leading to an even better result than if they posted a positive review in the first place.

They may even thank you for helping resolve the issue on the phone and apologize for posting the negative review. If they mention the review in any way after you remedied the situation, you could ask them if they would be willing to update or respond to the review to make sure people know how seriously you take patient concerns and how it turned out for them. Use your best judgment.

When a patient updates or responds to their negative review, you get the best of both worlds: the impact of a lower star rating to bring your overall rating below the fake-looking perfect 5-star rating plus the benefit of a patient letting people know how everything turned into a positive or that it was all a misunderstanding.

Recently I had a situation in my office that caused a patient to write a negative review on Google and Yelp! As soon as I saw the posts, I reached out via text message as I was on a plane flying to California so I was unable to call her. Here was my text message to her:

> [Name], it is Dr. Tau, First off, I want to apologize to you … I was pushing you to make a decision thinking that being direct with you was something that you needed, and obviously it was not, and I am sorry that it offended you. Secondly, I wanted to let you know that after you left I contacted one of the higher ups at Invisalign to see if they can do me a favor and get your case out of expiration and reactivated, which would only cost you $250 and would allow you one last refinement.

This morning, I am flying to California and saw that you wrote a negative review on Google and Yelp!, so before I proceed any further, I wanted to check with you to see how you wanted me to proceed. If you don't want to see me any longer that is fine and I completely understand. You are more than welcome to see my associate, who is amazing, and you will love her. I have not gotten the approval yet, but like I said, before I push for it, I wanted to check with you first.

This was her response a few minutes later:

Hi Dr. Tau, thank you for reaching out to me. I appreciate the apology, and I'm glad you are open to listening to me. I'm happy to move forward with the refinement, as I never wanted to leave your practice. I think you have a wonderful office, and I'm so happy to see that you are addressing everything. Thank you.

What followed is what I see many times: Reviews were edited and ratings were changed. There was also a negative comment on Facebook that was deleted.

By handling it offline, you can fix the issue, and many times as you can see they either take the review down or edit the star rating. At the same time, you avert a potential PR nightmare.

This above scenario has occurred multiple times in my office and many other offices to which I have given advice, and this is the best way to handle these negative reviews. Take it offline, handle the issue, and hope the patient takes the review down or edits it. You have the best of both worlds in this case: a happier patient and a better review.

Bury the negatives with even more positives.

In February 2018, my hometown Philadelphia Eagles went up against the dreaded New England Patriots in the Super Bowl. On paper, the Eagles were not expected to win. They had lost their starting quarterback to injury and had never before won the Super Bowl.

The Patriots, on the other hand, had won five Super Bowls and had arguably the best quarterback of all time, Tom Brady, playing some of his best football of his career and throwing to a nearly unstoppable tight end, Rob Gronkowski, and a number of clutch receivers and running backs. They had won the Super Bowl the year before and two of the previous three years.

The Patriots' offense was a powerhouse. And while the Eagles' defense made some clutch plays, the Patriots' still scored 33 points. In the 51-year history of the Super Bowl, no team had ever scored 33 points or more and lost, that is until 2018, when the Eagles beat the Patriots 41–33.

Like sports, sometimes the best defense is a good offense, and that is my best advice for bad reviews. When someone leaves a bad review, first attempt to make things better by taking the conversation offline. Then stay on plan and collect as many reviews as you can to bury the review down on the page. Ten reviews or a few months later, the impact of the negative review will be minimal at best.

One caveat, though, is to avoid breaking the rules to bury it right away. Keep going with your plan to get real, positive reviews. If you end up getting too many reviews at once or break the rules by buying reviews, having team members submit fake reviews, or having real patients submit reviews while they are still in your office, the new reviews could disappear. Your entire practice listing could even be removed.

You can certainly ask a few extra people to submit reviews right away to not have the negative one appear first, second, or even third. But avoid the impulse to go crazy or violate the rules. Just stick to your plan, and you will minimize the impact in no time.

I want to repeat—the best defense to a negative review is simply more positives, no matter how angry you are. Here's a voicemail I received from a fellow dentist:

> Hey, Len, Wayne here. Just got a review on Google from someone who's never been to my office, and it's a total bogus review. How do I deal with that crap? One star and a total lie about a story of coming into my office never been there no one by that name. How do you get this off? I'm actually prepared to file a lawsuit against this [bleep].

But such immediate anger goes away, as does the irrationality of suing someone over a negative review. Don't give in to your anger. Instead, bury the negative with more positives.

If you must respond, make sure you do not inadvertently violate HIPAA.

If you ask people what you should do when someone leaves you a negative review, at least five in 10 will suggest carefully responding. It is dangerous, and I highly recommend not doing that except in very rare circumstances. But if you really want to respond, be sure you do not end up like the dentist I mentioned above. In fact, even seemingly innocent responses can cross the line. Take this exchange, for example, where a patient mentioned specifics about their treatment in a positive review and a practice replied confirming some of the specifics:

★★★★★ 10 months ago - ⚐

Dr. Tom came highly recommended by quite a few of my coworkers. Each one who has been under his anesthesia showed and told me of their personal professional encounter with this doctor. I gave him a visit and I am so glad I did. Dr. Tom has provided professional, sanitary, and pain free dental work. He performed a root canal, fillings, crown, closed the gap between front teeth, tooth extraction, and is preparing and fitting my mouth for upper and lower partials, and will conclude with staining my teeth pearly white.

Thank you Dr. Tom and your dental assistance. Great Work!

 3

Response from the owner 10 months ago

Thanks Dwight. Your case is going really well. Glad we could close that gap in your front teeth for you today. Next time you come in, tell us what your friends and family think of your brand new smile. Please help us spread the word, everyone with ERISA/City of Austin insurance gets dental work done for free.

That is dangerous. It is much better practice to take the conversation offline, both with positive or negative situations. If you choose to respond, a general response is more appropriate.

I want to clarify something since there seems to be a lot of confusion over this topic. Confirming reviewers visited your office in and of itself is not a HIPAA violation as they are the ones that are basically saying they are a patient by writing a review. As I mentioned earlier, when you do respond, make sure you apologize and thank them for their feedback and mention your goal is to provide VIP experiences to everyone who interacts with your practice, and that anything that falls below that standard is unacceptable. Then ask them to contact you directly so you can get to the bottom of their concern and make things right.

"It is generally much more shameful to lose a good reputation than never to have acquired it."

—Pliny the Elder

Here is a good response to a negative review: "Thank you for your feedback about your experience at our office. We do apologize that you felt you were treated poorly, and we would like to discuss your concerns with you. Please contact the office so we can make amends and prevent it from happening in the future."

My oral surgeon had one of the best responses to a negative review recently. Here is how it played out:

2 reviews

★★☆☆☆ a year ago
Been waiting in the dr office for 50 mins, and was told I still have to wait a half hour more.

👍 Like

Here was the great response:

Response from the owner a year ago

I want to apologize and thank you for sharing your recent experience at our practice, ▮▮▮▮▮▮▮▮▮▮▮▮ We take great pride in providing each patient with the best quality of personalized care. Unfortunately on the day of your appointment our servers went down, delaying our surgeries and appointments.

We truly understand how valuable your time is and want to again apologize and thank you for your patience. We are actively working with our IT company to ensure unexpected disturbances to our servers do not happen again.

Although our collective apologies will not change your experience, I hope you find comfort in knowing your feedback was taken seriously.

Respectfully,

The dentist apologized multiple times and was empathetic about the patient waiting for such a long time and they even explained the reason why.

Another big takeaway from this review: Your patients can and will write a negative review while they are in the office waiting if you are running late.

Remember a perfect business is not one with perfect reviews; it's one that deals with feedback perfectly. You do want to avoid disclosing anything about a medical condition, as that is a HIPAA violation. If someone says they came in for a cleaning deal and were told they did not qualify for the deal and needed a more extensive deep cleaning, do not say anything about the condition. Stick to the same type of response as above.

Make sure everyone with access to respond knows what to say and what not to say. Have standard language they can copy and paste to avoid inadvertently revealing private health information or otherwise violating HIPAA.

I also would urge all dentists to relax, take a deep breath, and resist the urge to respond right away. If you are angry, you may not realize what you are writing, and that could have a dramatic impact on how you are perceived online. I don't like seeing angry responses on Yelp! It backfires every time.

Finally, it could be best to respond to all reviews—positive and negative ones—with HIPAA-compliant standard responses. While that could look cheesy, it also does not make the negative reviews stand out more by being the only ones with a response from the business, so it could be a better overall plan.

To recap, here are the dos and don'ts when it comes to handling negative reviews:

The Dos of Handling Negative Online Reviews

So, you know what to avoid when it comes to online reviews—that's the easy part. Now for what you should do when confronted with a negative online review.

1. Acknowledge the issue and apologize.

Just like in real life, most patients who complain on the internet simply want to be heard. Before you try to get to the bottom of the problem, it's crucial to empathize with them and apologize without blaming them. Show that you genuinely regret that a patient didn't leave your business on a positive note.

When you do apologize and explain the issue, you might change a customer's mind and turn the negative into a positive! In fact, 33% of negative reviews on Yelp! turn positive when you take the time to respond to the upset patient.

2. Tactfully promote a positive image of your business.

Without sounding like you're contradicting the reviewer and being argumentative, convey why his or her experience is rare in sincere and non-condescending language. If it feels natural, include some of your business's strengths in your reply. Responses can be a great way to flip the script and frame your business in a positive light—while still making the customer feel heard.

3. Be authentic and personal.

You never want to come off like you're giving a canned response. You or any employees who respond to negative online reviews should use real names (or first name and last initial) to explain your role in the business and give your direct phone number or email so they are able to reach back out to your offline. (Be careful who gets permission to post on your behalf, similar to the way I handle who has administrator access on my Facebook page.)

When it comes to replying to negative reviews, sincerity is the key. The easiest way to be authentic is to reach out to a patient on a personal level. The more authentic the response you give, the better it appears.

4. Take it offline.

To avoid an online exchange that everyone can see, you should always strive to take the discussion of the issue offline and then leave a sincere, thought-out public comment if at first you don't succeed.

If it feels right, taking the issue offline shows that you're fully willing to handle this situation—and you're not just apologizing for show.

The Biggest "Do" of All

Once you've dealt with the situation appropriately, *do* use negative reviews as a learning experience.

"Be more concerned with your character than your reputation, because your character is what you really are, while your reputation is merely what others think you are."

—John Wooden

If you consistently receive negative reviews or if a lot of reviews cite the same criticism—such as always running late or a problematic team member—something's up. This isn't just a one-off blip.

I recently had a conversation with an office that was struggling with negative reviews. When I read the reviews, they seemed to focus on the front desk person being rude. When I told the dentist he needed to change the person at the front desk, he told me he could not—*it was his wife.*

Obviously, the problems run deeper in this case, but you have to decide how to handle it when issues come up. Consistently negative reviews mean that it's time to make a change. Consider it free market research!

The Don'ts of Handling Negative Online Reviews

1. Get defensive.

It's natural to get mad when someone criticizes your business, especially if you feel the complaint is unfounded. You try to run your business as best as possible, so a bad review can feel like an attack.

But responding in anger does no good—and might possibly spiral into a viral nightmare. No small-business owner wants to be the raging entrepreneur who couldn't handle negative feedback. Take some time to get your thoughts in order before you respond. Maybe even write yourself an email to review later, and see how your thoughts come across on screen.

If you feel as though the situation was a total miscommunication, it might be hard to sound genuinely apologetic and not defensive. Even if you were in the right, try not to rub that in the patient's face—it'll only make the situation worse.

2. Ignore it.

Ignoring a negative online review is almost as bad as posting an expletive-filled answer. First, the reviewer will feel completely justified in his or her anger because you're not addressing the issue.

Second, other patients and potential patients will start to wonder if you really care, or if they can expect the same brush-off if they have a bad experience.

Being unresponsive on a bad review might signal to current and future customers that you really don't care about customer service, and situations like these aren't all that uncommon for your business.

If you try to reach out offline, then feel free to respond simply with a statement such as: "We are sorry you were not happy with your experience in our office. We have tried to call you but have been unable to reach you. Please call us to discuss your concerns. We want to ensure all of our patients are happy."

3. Get pulled into an online battle.

No matter how polite your initial response, you may run into a troll who just wants to keep complaining online. Here is an office that had an issue with a troll who continuously posted a similar review under different names. If you tried to reply to each of the troll's reviews, it could make things worse. It's best just to let it go and bury them with positive reviews.

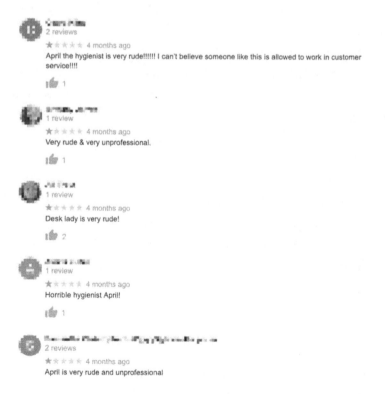

If your interaction threatens to escalate into an exchange of name-calling, just restate that you're happy to resolve the issue and ask the person to contact you offline. Other readers will see that you're being reasonable and that the troll isn't. But if you engage with someone who just wants to pick a fight, other quality customers might think you're just as petty as the complainer.

4. Beg for positive reviews to hide the negative ones.

If you fall victim to Don't No. 2 and ignore a negative, be sure to stay away from this one: hiding negative reviews by begging patients to give you positive ones. Of course, I work with BirdEye, but begging for a review and asking for feedback are two different things.

The best reviews for your business are those written by customers who were naturally compelled to gush about how great your business is. So if you have to pull teeth to get people to say great things about your business, it won't sound genuine on your review pages. And if you were asking for reviews to hide negative ones, patients will know what's up. If there are a bunch of fake-sounding positive reviews scattered between genuinely negative ones, odds are the patients will take the negative ones to heart.

Exercises

1. Talk with your team about the importance of getting regular reviews from happy patients and how the best defense to negative reviews is a good offense.

2. Make sure your team knows not to respond to negative reviews but to let you know when one comes up so you can personally reach out to the patient and take the conversation offline.

3. Resist the urge to respond to reviews, positive or negative. If you choose to respond, consider responding to both positive and negative reviews with HIPAA-compliant standard responses. Draft three or four samples of HIPAA-compliant responses to positive and negative reviews and keep them in a convenient

place for people to copy and paste in response to reviews to avoid inadvertent HIPAA violations.

CHAPTER 9

Creating a Reputation Culture for Your Office

All this information about local listings, social media, your website, earning a five-star reputation, collecting reviews, and reputation marketing is worthless if you do nothing with it.

To experience the benefits of all this information, your reputation marketing plan needs to be a core part of your practice culture. Here is how to build a reputation culture that sets you up to get found, get found in a compelling way, and collect and market online reviews from raving patients.

Get everyone on the same page.

The first step to creating a true reputation culture is to make sure every team member understands your reputation marketing strategy, why it is so important, and exactly what their role is.

That starts with explaining how local citations work and how optimizing them will help your practice rise up in Google's search results and attract more ideal patients. Keep all practice information, pictures, and videos in a folder with a list of the most important listing sites to update when anything changes.

If you use reputation marketing software such as BirdEye to help you keep everything consistent and updated on dozens of sites from one dashboard, make sure each team member involved in keeping things up to date knows how to update your information in the BirdEye dashboard so all your listing sites can be updated and consistent. I can even schedule a demo to show your team exactly how easy it is to do that. Just email me at Len@DrLenTau.com or call my cell at (215) 292-2100. I would be happy to help.

Second, discuss with your team how important it is to treat patients like VIPs and that the best way to set yourself up to receive five-star reviews is to treat everyone in a way that *deserves* a five-star review.

Third, make collecting and marketing reviews easy on yourself and your team. Train your team to ask patients for feedback and let them how that you read every one. Put everything they need to send review requests in one place so they can just copy and paste the follow-up messages. Let them know what to do with the positive reviews collected, such as taking screenshots of them or copying and pasting them into a document you can use to share on social media and on your website.

As with local citations, if you choose to use reputation marketing software to integrate with your practice management software and automate sending the requests, sharing the reviews, and building a microsite to help you control a top Google search result, walk them through the software so they can understand how it works. Again, if you need help training them, just reach out to me. I am happy to help.

One of the ways I recommend you get everybody on board with having a reputation culture is by offering the team an incentive when you first start making reputation a priority in your office. Most reviews do not mention any of the individual team members. Normally you see something like, "Dr. Tau and his staff are great." What makes reviews even more powerful is when individual team members get mentioned. I would recommend having a contest, and whoever can get their name mentioned in the review the most wins a prize, perhaps a day at the spa. I recommend a day at the spa as an incentive. You will make your team members happy, and they will certainly help generate more reviews from your patients.

Start every day with a focus on your five-star reputation.

I hold a brief huddle at the beginning of each day in my office. During the morning huddle, we talk about what is going on that day. I also reiterate how important it is to treat every person we interact with as a VIP and remind people to ask for feedback and let patients know we look forward to reviewing them.

If I am speaking at a conference or not in town for some other reason, my team holds the meeting without me. Either way, my entire office starts every day off with a reminder of how important our patients are and what we need to do to earn and collect a regular flow of positive online reviews.

Measuring the Impact of a Reputation Culture

No matter how much you focus on earning and collecting reviews, only a small percentage of patients will follow through and leave you reviews. That is okay, though, because you do not need thousands of reviews to be effective. A regular flow of positive reviews is all you need.

At the time of writing, my practice has more than 1,650 reviews, approximately 235 of which are on Google. Our average star rating is 4.8 stars.

But I have been focused on reputation marketing and collecting reviews for almost a decade. I have even used reputation marketing software to make the process easy for my team, first developing and using my iSocialReviews software before transitioning to BirdEye to help maintain consistent local citations and automate review collection and promotion.

Even with all that focus and automation, I still only average less than a handful of reviews each week. But a handful of reviews each week is all I have needed to regularly attract dozens of new patients each and every month from Google searches and my reputation marketing activities.

I know because I ask every new patient how they found me. Almost without fail, new patients mention using Google and reading online reviews before making an appointment. Even many of the ones who were referred by friends and family tell me they first searched Google and read reviews before making a final decision to make an appointment with me.

Even specialists who have always relied on referrals understand the power and the need for online reviews. When I refer a patient to a specialist, they don't just pick up the phone and call. They actually look them up online to see what others are saying about the office before they decide whether to use the specialist or choose someone else.

Welcome to the 21st century. Times have certainly changed.

In just a few minutes a day and BirdEye's reputation marketing software helping me automate, I regularly attract dozens of new patients each month.

Exercises

1. Let everyone on your team know the importance of creating a reputation culture in your office. Talk with them about what files, tools, and resources you have to make things easier for them. Reiterate how much better patient experience will be with a reputation culture.

2. If you choose to use software like BirdEye to help you automate and maintain consistency, schedule personalized training with me so you do not have to worry about training your team on

how the software works. Just email me at Len@DrLenTau.com or call my cell at (215) 292-2100. I would be happy to help.

3. Start your next workday with a morning huddle, where you reiterate the importance of a reputation culture and what it takes to earn a five-star reputation. If you already have systems in place for collecting and marketing reviews, remind your team of where they can find everything they need to collect reviews and what to do with reviews as they come in. If you have incentivized your team, remind them of the incentive and what they have to do to earn it.

4. Visit the resources page at DrLenTau.com/BookResources and scroll to the resources for this chapter. You will find several resources there to help you make creating a reputation culture easier.

CONCLUSION AND INVITATION

In a world dominated by Google, Facebook, Twitter, Pinterest, Instagram, and online reviews, we dentists have two choices when it comes to our marketing.

We can keep doing what worked in the 1990s (and earlier), or we can use the internet to our advantage, optimize our local citations, earn a five-star reputation, and then collect and distribute raving patient reviews from our raving patients.

The Problem with Marketing Like It's 1999

While it might be fun to *party* like it's 1999, marketing your dental practice like it's 1999 won't be very fun.

You'll spend way too much money and work way too hard to get patients to your practice.

You'll be virtually invisible online—where almost every patient looks before choosing a dentist. Whether they're searching for a dentist in your area or checking you out after a friend or family member mentions you, the vast majority of patients will search for you on Google before making an appointment.

If your website looks old and your online presence is poor, it's highly likely they'll look for another dentist.

Why Reputation Marketing Is the Solution

Word-of-*mouth* no longer leads directly to new patients. The vast majority of time, people at least make a pit stop online before choosing a dentist. They check social media and they check search engines, especially Google.

In the new word-of-*mouse* world, as I call it, we *must* meet patients where they are, and that's online.

This can be done one of two ways. We can spend thousands of dollars on paid advertising, or we can use reputation marketing to optimize our local citations, earn and collect glowing patient reviews, and then send those reviews everywhere our future patients are.

The former can be effective in the short term or if you have specific high-revenue procedures you want to promote, such as I do with Invisalign patients in Philadelphia or as other dentists do to promote their dental implant practice.

Paid advertising can get you on the top of Google search results right away. But it will be costly and put you at the mercy of Google's advertising rates. If you do go this route, such campaigns are most effective when you have a nice foundation of reviews. So, it comes back to the same assessment: In order to grow your business, you need lots of social proof, which begins with reviews, reviews, and more reviews.

"A good reputation is more valuable than money."

—Publulius Syrus

A more reliable and effective long-term plan is to implement a true reputation marketing plan. You can get started for free or use true reputation marketing software to automate and ensure consistency. Even using software to help, your entire marketing costs will be a *fraction* of what you'd need to pay for an effective paid marketing campaign. And unlike paid marketing, if you decide to no longer use the software, your local citations and reviews don't disappear.

The choice is yours.

You can worry about what people will see if they Google you or whether anyone will even find you when they're searching for a dentist.

Or you can take control of your online reputation and ensure you'll not only be *found* when people are looking for a dentist but be found in a way that builds immediate trust and actually gets patients in your chair.

When I first bought my dental practice, I made the choice to take control and consistently attract dozens of new patients every month. I've helped *thousands* of other dentists do the same using the exact plan I've just outlined for you.

I hope you use this system to build raving patients and become the next great reputation marketing success story. You work way too hard to worry about one-star reviews or how you are going to find your next patient.

If you need help, don't forget to check the resources page at DrLenTau.com/BookResources. Or, just email me at Len@DrLenTau. com, or call or text my cell at (215) 292-2100. I'm passionate about helping dentists make their businesses stronger and their lives better. Even though I have been nicknamed the Reviews Doctor or the BirdEye Guy (thanks, Glenn Vo) I do have a lot of experience helping practices take their practice to the next level using the internet and online marketing. If you want to see how I can help you, go to DrLenTau.com/dymo for a free report that shows how you stand online and where you can improve.

And always remember these two words: Reputation Matters.

ACKNOWLEDGMENTS

Sometimes people write books to transform and change lives, sometimes people write books to inform and educate, and sometimes people write books to share their message.

I have dreamed about writing this book (which I hope does all three of the above) for a long time, and the only reason you have it in your hands is because of the contributions of a number of people.

I would like to thank all of the people who contributed stories about reputation, advice about reviews, and expert opinions.

Here they are, in no particular order: coach Heidi Mount; Robin Bethell from Forest Family Dentistry; Pete Johnson from Get Practice Growth; Evan Lazarus from Simple Impact Media; Justin Morgan, the Dental Marketing Guy; Dr. Joanne Block Reif from Crossroads Dental Arts in Owing Mills, Maryland; dental consultant Minal Sampat; Rita Zamora from Rita Zamora Connections; Susan Leckowicz from Dental Coaches; Dr. Nathan Ho from Affinity Smiles in Roanoke, Texas, and CEO of Envision Stars; Dr Anissa Holmes, founder of Delivering WOW; and Dr. Glenn Vo, creator of NiftyThriftyDentists.com.

Thank you for making this book a better one. Your contributions are greatly appreciated.

Thank you to my wonderful wife, Risa, whose patience, dedication, support, and love have allowed me to shift my career from full-time clinical dentistry to part-time clinical dentistry, speaking, consulting, and writing. Without your support, none of this would be possible. I love you.

Thank you to Nick Pavlidis and Authority Ghostwriting. (I know you are not necessarily supposed to acknowledge the person who helped you get the book to the finish line, but I did use a ghostwriter since I would have never been able to finish it on my own.). Nick used all of my seminars, articles, and podcasts to help write this book with my own words, editors Sarah Tuff Dunn and Ethan Webb updated and polished the content, and Jennifer Harshman reviewed the manuscript to make sure it was clean and consistent. Thanks, Nick, for answering your phone when I needed advice, making sure I got things to you by the deadline, and helping me finish *Raving Patients*.

To all of my patients, clients, and attendees of my seminars—you are the reason I do what I do. The results speak for themselves.

ABOUT THE AUTHOR

Chosen as one of the top leaders in dental consulting by *Dentistry Today*, Len Tau, DMD, has dedicated his professional life to improving dentistry for both patients and other dentists.

After purchasing his practice, the Pennsylvania Center for Dental Excellence in Philadelphia in 2007, Len practiced full-time while consulting to other dental practices, training thousands of dentists about reputation marketing, leading the dental division of BirdEye, a reputation marketing platform, and hosting the popular, *Raving Patients* podcast.

In 2018, Len cut down to practicing dentistry two days per week to focus additional time and attention to helping other dentists build broad and compelling online footprints that attract hundreds of new patients to their practices.

Len lectures nationally and internationally on using internet marketing, social media, and reputation marketing to make dental offices more visible and credible as well as how to increase their case acceptance.

In addition to being the General Manager of the Dental Division for BirdEye, Len is the founder of Tau Dental Consulting, a consulting firm that helps dentists develop a comprehensive online marketing plan.

His content-rich, engaging seminars allow him to bring his firsthand experiences to his audiences. He lives in Blue Bell, Pennsylvania with his wife, Risa, and son, Aidan.

To connect with Len, visit DrLenTau.com, email him at Len@DrLenTau.com, or just text or call him on his cell.